THE YANKEE SCRIMSHANDERS

THE YANKEE SCRIMSHANDERS

by

FREDRIKA ALEXANDER BURROWS

WILLIAM S. SULLWOLD PUBLISHING
TAUNTON, MASSACHUSETTS

Library of Congress Catalogue Number 73-80907

Printed in the United States

Contents

Illustrations

Hugo G. Poisson — Photographer

Foreword

The stories, facts and figures of The Golden Age of Whaling have taken their places in the history books. The last wind-driven whaling ship is presently berthed in a museum, and whaling ports, once alive and teeming with the sights and sounds of arriving and departing whaleships, are now marinas for expensive yachts and motorized pleasure craft.

The men who took part in this exciting and romantic era, however, have increased in stature with the passing of time, and become legendary. The Yankee scrimshander was, first and foremost, a whaleman. A pioneer with innate seamanship, fearless, stoic, and enterprising, he sailed the Seven Seas, explored and charted new sea lanes to the four corners of the earth, and built up an industry, with its dependent industries, that affected the economy and progress of an entire nation.

The adventures of these 'iron men and wooden ships' continue to fascinate young and old alike, and the souvenirs and memorabilia of their lives at sea while pursuing whales, are viewed with awe and admiration. All that remains of that strenuous, dangerous and exciting era, however, is a street of magnificent mansions on Nantucket Island (built with the profits made by prosperous ship owners), artifacts now enshrined in whaling museums, and pieces of scrimshaw which, even at the present time, continue to be discovered in New England attics.

Scrimshaw — the etchings, carvings, and contrivances of the Yankee scrimshanders — has become the most eagerly sought collectible of Americana. It has been estimated that, during the one hundred or more years in which whaling was vigorously pursued, some twenty thousand New England and New York whalemen spent their leisure time in fashioning hundreds of thousands of pieces of scrimshaw. Brought home in their pockets and sea chests, this handwork was a mute reminder of long and arduous voyages endured in following the whale, of the endless days and weeks of waiting to sight and pursue them.

7

The bulk of the drawings in scrimshaw are the recordings by the sailors themselves of the activities, customs, and life-styles of a period of about forty years, 1825-1865, called 'The Golden Age of Whaling'. This span of years saw the rise and decline of an industry and its numerous dependent industries, and the end of a way of life that affected the Eastern Seaboard from Baltimore, Maryland, to Portland, Maine, and the offshore islands.

In order to understand and appreciate the Yankee scrimshander and his folk art it is necessary to have a brief description of whales, whaleships, whalemen and their environment.

A Whaling Song

Bold, hardy men with blooming age
Our sandy shores produce,
With monstrous fish they do engage
And dangerous callings choose.

Dr. John Osborne

Appreciation

I wish to express my appreciation and heartfelt thanks to all those who gave so generously of their time, for valuable assistance in procuring material and pictures, for making available documents and other subject matter on whales, whalemen, and whale fishery, and for their lively interest in the progress of this book.

To: Ms. Elizabeth Tyrer, Nantucket Historical Association; Philip F. Purrington, Old Dartmouth Historical Society Whaling Museum; Philip C. F. Smith, Peabody Museum; Ms. Virginia Ewalt, Mystic Seaport; Walter B. Stearns, Suffolk County Whaling Museum; Frederick P. Schmitt, Whaling Museum, Cold Spring Harbor; Nelson O. Price, H. R. Bradley Smith, Theodore F. Amaral, Heritage Plantation; Joseph Smart, Cape Cod Community College; Ms. Grace Chesbro, Osterville Historical Association; Ms. Eleanor Yeager, Falmouth Historical Association; Reverend Harry Clarke, Yarmouth Port Historical Association; to the capable and interested staffs at the Falmouth, Hyannis, Osterville and Sandwich libraries; to Houghton Mifflin Company for permission to quote from John A. Cook's *Pursuing The Whale;* to Ms. Kathryn C. Diddell for quotation from *Bertha Goes Whaling* by Ms. Bertha Boyce; to Richard A. Bourne, Richard A. Bourne Company, Inc.; Robert Lavery, K. B. Kittredge, Ms. Janice Glover, John J. Mitchell, Dr. George Ross Starr, Lawrence E. Vienneau, Jr.; to the Twelve O'Clock Scholars for assistance and encouragement; and especially to Ron Burrows, whose advice, encouragement and sharing of his great fund of knowledge on the subject has been invaluable.

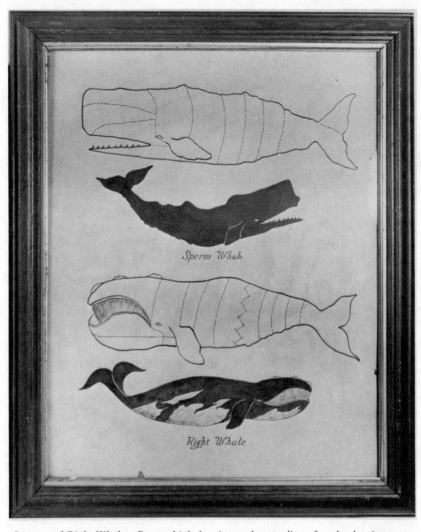

Sperm and Right Whale – Pen and ink drawing and an outline of each, showing pattern for spiral cutting of the blubber. Courtesy Richard A. Bourne Co. Inc.

I   Whales and Whale Fishery

"Oh, the rare old whale, 'mid storm and gale,
In his ocean home will be
A giant in might where might is right,
And King of the boundless sea."

Whale fishery has had an important place in American history, in its industrial, physical and social development. It began with the settlement of the colonies, when whales were used as food, then became a definite income-producing industry when the commercial value of whale oil and bone was realized.

The first whaling expeditions in this country were undertaken in small boats that traveled coastwise. In those days whales were plentiful off shore, often seen by those remaining on land, waiting for the monster to be brought ashore where they would cut off its blubber and try it out in furnaces which they erected on the beach.

In a book of poems by William Morrell of Plymouth which was published in London in 1623 we find —

"The mighty whale doth in theses harbors lye,
Whose Oyle the mearchant deare will buy."

Although the pursuance and capturing of whales is called 'whale fishery', the whale is, indeed, not a fish, but a mammal. It is warm-blooded, has an animal bone structure, produces its young live and suckles it.

But the whales differ so widely from other mammals in all aspects of their biology, that a specialized branch of zoology, called cetology (from the Order Cetacea to which the whales belong) has evolved.

Some of the interesting questions which arise, and are yet to be resolved, in the study of whales are — How do they communicate with their own kind? By what mechanisms do they navigate the world's oceans and return to their spawning grounds the next season? How are they able to make rapid dives to depths of a mile, or more, where pressures should be enough to crush the whale's ribs, and then return quickly to the surface without suffering the "bends" which can cripple, and sometimes kill, a human if he ascends too rapidly from only a fraction of that depth? How do whales handle oxygen and carbon dioxide during long periods of submersion? What is their social structure and organization?

Solving these questions will take time, but does the scientist have enough time? The important immediate question for us, as ecologists and world citizens interested in the preservation of the whale species is — Can we achieve international cooperation in regulating laws on whale fishery before hunters deplete the species and they become, in ever diminishing numbers, finally extinct?

Whales have always been objects of wonder and awe. Milton wrote in *Paradise Lost*: "That sea beast / Leviathon which God of all His works / Created hughest that / Swim the ocean stream."

Unless you have seen a dead whale which has been cast upon the beach and left there by the outgoing tide, which happens occasionally on Cape Cod and other shores near whaling grounds, you cannot possibly imagine the enormousness of the creatures. The largest animal ever known, in size or strength, the whale is often referred to as a 'leviathon'. A whale, ninety feet long and weighing approximately seven tons, is said to have a mouth twenty-five feet long and fifteen feet high. With dimensions of such proportions the story of Jonah and the whale becomes completely believable.

Scotch-born Ivan T. Sanderson discusses the sizes of different whales in his book *Follow The Whale* and tells of wriggling, at the age of nine years, through the main artery of a seventy foot right whale into its heart, to amuse a group of sailors.

There are several kinds of whales, all of which yield oil, but we are concerned with only two in the production of whale oil, whale bone and its by-product — scrimshaw. These are the sperm (toothed) whale and the right whale (no teeth).

The sperm whale, or cachalot, is the largest of the toothed

whales. It is a warm water animal and, as such, swims, migrates and breeds within the limits of south temperate seas. This accounts for the fact that American whaleships were found off the coasts of Chili, Peru, Fiji, Sandwich, the Azores, Galapagos, and the Cape Verdes.

The structure of the sperm is distinctly different from that of the toothless, or baleen, whales. It has an enormous square head which constitutes one third of its body. This vast tank contains approximately one ton of light oil, the type desirable to burn in lamps, as it burns away without leaving a residue (lampblack) on the wicks. It was, and is, the basis for the finest machine oil.

At the base of this tremendous cavity is a layer of wax-like oil, called spermaceti, which was used for candles, ointments and cosmetics. Some of the larger sperms have yielded as much as twenty-four barrels of this tallow-like substance. The blubber was reduced to oil for ordinary purposes in huge try-pots. It should be noted, also, that an added reward was always hoped for in the form of ambergris, — a substance found in the intestines of diseased whales, which was used as a fixative in perfume and brought unbelievably high prices.

Right whales, given this name because they were the 'right' whales to hunt (larger yield), were called the 'whalebone' whales. Curiously, too, their oil is 'whale oil', while that of the sperm whale is 'sperm oil'.

Larger and more fierce than sperms, the right whales live in cold water, (some whaling expeditions pushed up the northwest coast to the Arctic), which makes their blanket of blubber thicker. They were also hunted for baleen, a stiff horn-like material that grows down in plates from the roof of their mouth. These plates number from 300 to 500, are about ten feet long and are set one-fourth inch apart. They run parallel to one another, terminating on the inner edge of the mouth in a hairy fringe.

Right whales swim with their mouths open, scooping up tons of water and small fish. The suspended baleen acts as a sieve, allowing only food of a particular size to enter the comparatively small throat of the whale.

In the book *Moby Dick* Herman Melville describes the mouth of the right whale thus:

"The roof is about twelve feet high, and runs to a pretty sharp angle, as if there were a regular ridge-pole there; while these ribbed, arched, hairy sides present us with those wondrous half vertical, scimitar-shaped slats of whalebone, — say three hundred on a side, which depending from the upper part of the head or crown bone, form those Venetian blinds. The edges of these bones are fringed with hairy fibers through which the Right Whale strains water, and in whose intricacies he retains small fish, when, open-mouthed, he goes through the seas of brit in feeding time.''

The product baleen was used in various articles, as buggy whips, umbrella and parasol spokes, corset stays, fishing rods, shoe horns, combs, brushes, hoops (for hoop skirts), in fact anything that needed stiffening, yet would also bend. It was not until pliable steel was invented that the baleen, or right whale, industry was abandoned.

"Rare sailor's model of the 'Andrew Hicks' ", complete with rigging, whaleboats, etc. 'Andrew Hicks' was a 303 tonnage bark built in Westport, Mass. in 1867. Courtesy Richard A. Bourne Co. Inc.

II Whaleships and Whaleboats

As whales grew scarce in the vicinity of the shores and whale fishery became increasingly prosperous, being protected by a Massachusetts law enacted in 1639 which exempted those taking whales from a tax for seven years, more and larger ships were built. By 1843 Nantucket had eighty-eight ships out pursuing whales.

Heavier ships caused the demise of the whale oil industry on Nantucket, however, as a sand bar in her harbor was a barrier to the larger whale ships and, by 1857, New Bedford had taken over supremacy of the whaling industry. At that time New Bedford numbered 329 ships from her deeper and more navigable harbor.

Ship owners of those days were the real pioneers of industry, establishing whole communities dedicated to ship building and its resulting prosperity through the products of whale fishery and through foreign trade. Ship after ship was built; they sailed to the four corners of the world, for the most part successfully, often with harrowing experiences.

Small towns near seaports benefited from ship building and its accompanying industries. Many of the vessels built in neighboring communities were manned by local sailors although their papers were drawn up in the whaling ports of Nantucket and New Bedford.

Rochester, Massachusetts, was one of these, its harbor able to accommodate the smaller ships. The Reverent Thomas Robbins, pastor of the Second Church of Christ, described the town's happenings in his diary. An excerpt from 1839 reads:

Apr. 4 News came that the brig *Annawan* of this place, coming home with a valuable cargo, was wrecked near Bermuda, and the men are reported missing. Several families are much distressed.

Apr. 15 Painful news received here this morning from the brig *Annawan*, wrecked. Of 21 of the crew, 14, including the captain and mates, are lost; 7 saved, 7 from this place; 4 lost. The cargo worth about $20,000.00.

Apr. Saw a seaman Chase, who was wrecked in the *Annawan*. His story was very affecting. Four promising youths of this place were lost.

May 10 A whale brig came in here that has done well.

May 17 Yesterday a whale brig came in with 600 bbls. of sperm oil.

Aug. 9 A ship from this place with 2000 bbls. of oil has been lost in the Indian Ocean; men saved. A severe loss.

Aug. 21 A whale brig sailed from here.

Aug. 27 A fine ship was launched here this morning.

Oct. 7 It is supposed we have lost a schooner from this place; a good vessel with its crew, on their passage from Philadelphia to Boston in the disastrous storm of Aug. 30.

Nov. 7 A whale brig came in here last night after a very prosperous voyage.

Whaleships were the most strongly-built vessels afloat, — and for good reason — they had to be to endure the hardships of the sea which they encountered, — the storm-lashed waters of Cape Horn, the hurricane winds of the Pacific, the crushing ice of the Arctic. Staggering under mountains of sail and weighted down with the tremendous loads which they must carry, they plowed the uncharted seas in search of the whale and returned with their harvest.

Bulky and sea-worthy, whalers were high bulwarked and blunt-bowed. Copper-fastened and sheathed they were all square-rigged, averaging from 100-125 feet in length and ranging between 200 and 500 tons. Specific types of vessels used were the schooner, the bark and the ship.

The schooner, the smallest of the three, had two masts and was rigged fore and aft. It was used for shorter trips, carrying a crew of about sixteen men. The bark was three masted, with a foremast and mainmast square-rigged, the mizzenmast fore and aft rigged. It carried between 250 and 400 tons and a crew of from sixteen to twenty-four men.

The ship was the largest whaling vessel used and required a full compliment of crew and equipment. Ships had three masts, — mainmast, foremast and mizzenmast, — each having lower mast, top mast and top gallant mast. Rigged to withstand violent and heavy strains, and averaging between 300 and 500 tons, they had the ability to carry a full cargo of oil together with whaling gear and tryworks, a crew of twenty-four men, with food and supplies for a period of from two to four years.

Before setting out for each expedition a whaleship was gone over and re-conditioned from stem to stern. No detail was overlooked in preparing a ship for another hazardous voyage, for, not only was the safety of the ship at stake, but the lives of the men in her crew and the assurance of a successful "greasy" voyage. Shipwrights scraped and re-coppered the hull; ships' carpenters and caulkers made the necessary repairs below the water line, riggers tested, repaired and replaced masts and sails, coils of hemp, tackle blocks and fluke chains, strained and wrenched by plunging seas.

The implements and tools were sharpened, re-inforced and replaced in order of use, supplies brought on board and checked. Nothing could be left to chance because, except for an occasional stop-over at a Chilean port or South Pacific isle for water and fresh fruit, all food and medicinal supplies must be carried with them.

Terrific strain was put on the ship when a whale was captured, brought along side and lashed to the ship for dissection and processing. The decks served as landing platforms for the "cutting-in" and storage of bone to be cleaned. The blubber was rendered in 250 gallon iron try-pots over works erected on the deck forward of the fore hatch.

The try-works were a furnace constructed of bricks and iron, with open frame work, and a flat top large enough to hold two iron cauldrons (try pots). When the blubber had been reduced to oil it was drawn off through spigots, and allowed to cool, then poured into barrels and stored below deck. Remnants of blubber and carcass left in the pots were thrown on the fire for hotter and faster fuel.

Fire was an ever present danger and precaution against it was taken by erecting a foot-high trough around the blazing furnace in which sea water was always kept.

Many ships never returned and countless numbers of lives were lost in pursuing the whale, but the majority of those that did return were heavily laden, and richly rewarded the efforts of those who had invested time, labor and money in them.

Five whaleboats were considered a necessity on a whaleship. Hung from davits, these boats were double-ended 30 feet long and six feet wide, with a depth of 22 inches midships and 37 inches at the bow and stern. Three whaleboats were slung on the port side of the ship, one on the starboard quarter, another on the starboard bow. Built for speed, stoutness and sea-worthiness they were said to be able to 'ride the heaviest sea, withstand the highest wind, and resist the heaviest gale'. Sailors, having of necessity to abandon ship, often spent days in these boats waiting to be rescued, or endeavoring to reach a distant shore. They depended on the durability and sea-fitness of the whaleboat.

Each whaleboat was manned by six men, — the "boatsteerer", who handled the front oar and wielded the harpoon; the officer called the "boatheader", who killed the whale with the lance, and four oarsmen.

Seldom were more than two boats used at one time in pursuing, harpooning and capturing the whale (unless two whales were in the vicinity at the same time), but "a dead whale or a stove boat" was often a harsh reality, and it was wise to carry enough equipment. This included harpoons, lances, hatchet, boat spade, knives, drinking water and medicine. Two tubs of line were stored, one fore and one midship, 225 and 75 fathoms long. The lines could be spliced for extra length. The whale often sounded to great depth when struck.

Sometimes the monster would 'run' instead of diving, in which case the sailors had a 'Nantucket sleigh ride', and just hung on until the whale tired. This was the most exciting and terrifying experience in whale taking and furnished many a lively tale on a winter night back home by the fire.

One sole survivor of the whaling fleet, under sail, remains. The *Charles W. Morgan,* built in New Bedford and named after one of the most successful whaling merchants of the time, is now berthed at a wharf at Mystic Seaport, a marine museum at Mystic, Connecticut. Here she offers the interested and curious visitor an opportunity to walk her decks and dream dreams of whaling days and derring do.

In active service for eighty years, the *Morgan* made thirty-seven voyages, cruising the Arctic and Antarctic, the Atlantic and Pacific, the Okhotsk and Japan Seas, and the Indian Ocean. She traversed more miles and took more whales than any other whaleship while enduring the trials and hardships common to whale fishery. She weathered two hurricanes, was struck by lightning three times, was driven ashore at least once, saw several mutinies and was once set afire by her crew.

The *Morgan's* final whaling voyage took place in September 1920 at eighty years of age, returning to the home port of New Bedford in May 1921 with 700 barrles of sperm oil in her hold.

Built by master shipwrights with live oak, copper-fastened, rigged with the stoutest hemp and manila rope, by workmen who took pride in their work, longevity was the rule, rather than the exception, for whaleships, and each one was a credit to an industry important to the progress of America.

The Whaler's Song

> Spout / Spout / Spout /
> The waves are purling all about;
> Every billow on its head
> Strangely wears a crest of red.
> See her lash the foaming main
> In her fury and her pain.
>   Take good heed, my hearts of oak,
> Lest her flukes, as she lies,
> Swiftly hurl you to the skies.
>   But lo / her giant strength is broke.
> Slow she turns, as a mass of lead, —
> The mighty mountain whale is dead.

(Author unknown)

III Whalemen

Danger, excitement, perilous adventure, — no wonder the siren call of whaling attracted young men from all over New England and upper New York state. If one were to believe the pictures on the works of art brought back by whaling crews, reproductions of their own experiences, every voyage was a duplicate of the 19th century thriller, *Moby Dick,* by Herman Melville, and every young man who followed a whaling career could look forward to a rewarding journey, financially, and excitement galore.

Strange as it may seem, the Biblical Jonah was not the only sailor to have had a hair-raising experience with a whale. A nineteenth century Jonah fell into the jaws of a sperm whale and lived to tell the story.

In 1864 Captain Peleg Nye of Barnstable, Massachusetts, was taken on as first mate on the schooner, *G. W. Lewis,* Holmes the captain, out of Provincetown, their destination the Atlantic whaling grounds. On this particular day a sperm whale was sighted off the bow and the sailors took to the boats. Following custom, Nye was the boatheader in one whaleboat, the captain in the other. The pursuit was a lively one, and upon gaining the side of the whale, the boatsteerer in Nye's boat was able to make fast the harpoon in the side of the whale, then exchanged places with Nye for the kill.

The whale turned to run, however, and struck the boat with its flukes, smashing the whaleboat and tossing its occupants into the water. Nye, standing in the prow of the boat, fell forward into the huge opened jaws of the leviathan and, before the horrified eyes of his companions, disappeared as the cavernous mouth closed.

20

The sperm whale has teeth on its lower jaws only, several inches apart, and it was between these teeth that the mate's legs were wedged. Mortally wounded, the animal dove with Nye encased in its mouth, but surfaced almost immediately. Gasping, it opened its jaws, permitting its unwilling occupant to dislodge his legs and escape into the water.

Despite several broken ribs, and teeth punctures in his back, Nye was able to swim to some pieces of the stove boat and hang on until the captain and crew in the other whaleboat could rescue him.

Another exciting story is told of the harpooner from Provincetown who rode on the back of a humpback whale. A hunt off the coast of Spain produced a whale which was pursued and struck with the harpoon by the boatsteerer. The enraged animal rushed the boat, spilling its occupants into rolling waves. The harpooner, thrown from a standing position, landed on the whale's back near the harpoon which was embedded in its flesh.

Dazed, but conscious of the need to save himself, the sailor grabbed the shaft of the upright harpoon and hung on while the whale made a run to escape its enemies. It circled and came back, perhaps with the intention of upsetting a second boat that was standing nearby. Holding the line which was still attached to the harpoon fastened in the whale's back, the rider slid off the slippery back and swam to the other boat.

The whale was eventually captured and killed, and the Cape Cod whaleman was no worse for his whale back ride.

Capturing and processing whales was hard and specialized work and necessitated the training of each new crew. Few 'enlistees' signed on for a second voyage. The 'regulars' consisted of the captain, the first and second mates (a boatheader was always an officer), three boatsteerers (harpooners), a cooper who also doubled as a blacksmith in many cases, and a cook. There were some seamen who were "pros", that is, who followed the sea and would not feel at home following a trade on land. The bulk of the crew, however, was made up of volunteers, — young men in their teens and early twenties, signed on for each expedition.

Bored with life in small inland towns or on the farms, lured by thrilling tales of adventure on the high seas, romance in the South Sea Isles and wealth from harvesting whale oil, these impressionable youths crowded into the seaports and signed for a 'lay' on a whaleship. Most of them had never even been in a row boat, knew nothing about sailing, the handling of sails or sailing gear. Most had never seen a whale.

It fell to the officers to train these green recruits; — how to handle sails, wield an axe and boat hooks, how to lower the whaleboats, handle the oars and pull in unison. Since it all had to be taught after they got under way, the basics were all they had time for, in some instances.

Captain DeBlois wrote in his journal aboard the *Ann Alexander* on June 9, 1850: — "Here we are, 8 days from home, and I am more homesick than ever before. The crue I cant tell much about yet. They are very green, most of them were sea sick."

These young men, the "crue", were quickly disillusioned. They found the life of a whaleman harsh, laborious, and, between whale taking, monotonous. The living conditions were crowded, the food abominable. On most ships the sleeping quarters were cramped, recreation and exercise areas non-existent.

One would expect that leisure time would be at a minimum on a whaleship, but the fact is, there were too many men for the size of the ship. They were needed at the time of capturing and processing whales and, although they had regular duties to perform in the upkeep and running of the ship (standing watch, taking turns as look-out, scrubbing the deck, keeping the equipment clean and in good working order, sails mended and ropes spliced), time hung heavy on their hands when not engaged in whale taking.

Because it was not profitable to return to home port without a full hold, voyages of three and four years were not unusual. Sailing vessels took months to get to whaling grounds, — some from New England went around Cape Horn into the Pacific, — often weeks and months went by before sighting a whale, more time to capture it and reduce it to barrels of oil and bundles of bone. Oftentimes it took twenty-five to thirty whales to fill a hold. Months and sometimes years went by before the ship was ready to return on the home trip.

The story is told of a whaleship captain, who upon boarding his vessel in New Bedford, was reminded that he had neglected to bid his wife "good-bye". To which he gruffly replied, "No need, only going to be gone a couple of years."

Under such adverse conditions you may wonder why so few men deserted or jumped ship. The reason was a logical one. When a man signed on as a member of the crew of a whaling vessel he did not sign for wages, as merchant seamen did, but for a 'lay'. This meant that in lieu of wages he would share in whatever profits were made from the expedition. Thus, if the ship made a 'greasy' voyage (full load of oil), all hands shared, percentage-wise, from the captain to the cabin boy. If the voyage were not successful, the crew realized the loss as well as the owner. Having an interest in the profits furnished the incentive to stay with the ship, to work hard and to endure the perils of whale fishery.

Profits on a whaling expedition were uncertain, however, even when a ship returned with a full hold. One of the risks which a whaleman faced was the price of oil when the cargo was sold.

On the day that the *Ann Alexander* reached port, November 4, 1849, having been out for four years, sperm was paying $1.15 and whale oil paying $.47 per gallon. Her load of 1243 barrels grossed $45,027.72. According to the lay decided upon at the beginning of the voyage and set forth in the shipping paper, the captain and crew received the following:

Isaac F. Sawtelle	Master 1/17	$2,648.69
John S. DeBlois	Mate 1/27	1,667.69
Orin B. Higgins	2nd Mate 1/45	1,000.61
Alfred Morse	3rd Mate 1/60	750.46
Charles Lakewood	Boatsteerer 1/80	562.84
Christopher Card	Cooper 1/60	750.46

Mariners', or ordinary seamen's allotments ranged between 1/120 or $375.23 and 1/260 or $281.42.

There were few opportunities to spend money and a sailor's lay could be clear profit, their living expenses provided while aboard ship. Some men did run up bills against their lays through gambling, buying liquor and gifts in foreign ports, and came home in debt, with nothing to show for four years of drudgery and hard work.

Sperm Teeth – Scrimshaw designs from Godey fashion prints. Author's Collection.

IV   Wives Of Whalemen

Though the captain was away the crew at home carried on as though he was present, — the first mate was the wife and the sailors, the children. All had duties to perform and chores to do. Daily results and accomplishments were to be logged, and reported when the whaleman returned to homeport.

The life of a wife, left ashore while her husband the whaler, was a lonely one, filled with anxiety, responsibility and hard work. It fell to her to carry on as business manager, keeping in touch with the ship owner, as well as home manager.

Capable, independent, intelligent and thrifty, the wives performed the rugged chores on the farms, raised their families, conducted businesses, keeping the business accounts as well as the home accounts. It was very important to keep well within the limits set up as a whaleman's share of the profits, (if the voyage proved unsuccessful they would have little with which to pay bills); they must support their familes from the produce of the farm, money in the form of cash being practically non-existant.

Some wives chose to share life aboard ship on the perilous ocean with their seafaring husbands. Sometimes a bride's honeymoon was her first voyage aboard a whaler, lasting from three to four years. Her children were born in lonely, far away places with strange-sounding names.

Whether wives were at home or aboard ship the sea dominated their lives. Born in coastal towns and raised in sea-faring families, they expected and accepted their lot. Of those wives who went to sea, many only settled down when their husbands retired, — generally to Cape Cod.

Azubah Bearse Handy, daughter of Bethuel G. Handy who captained a coastal schooner, was a seamstress in a Cotuit tailor shop when she met her future husband in September 1835. Attracted by a young man who came to the shop and ordered a suit of clothes, Azubah placed a note in a pocket of the finished suit: "I hope I meet the dashing young man I made these clothes for."

Intrigued, William Cash returned to the shop and made her acquaintance, but almost immediately shipped out as boatsteerer aboard the *Edward Quernell* of Fall River. In May 1839, thirty-five months later, homeward bound, a storm caught the ship, tossed it onto the shore at Long Island and smashed it. Only four sailors were saved, William being one of them.

He made his way to Cotuit and married Azubah, but after a few weeks rest he signed on as second mate on the ship *Ganges*. This vessel burned in port in Chile. Fortunately the *Milton*, out of New Bedford was in port and Cash obtained a berth as second mate on her. Their voyage into the North Pacific pursuing whales was successful and the ship returned to homeport on May 9, 1842.

William Cash had been away from home for two years and was welcomed back by a wife and son. He now had responsibilities, and set out May 28 as chief mate aboard the *Milton*, not returning until May 1847, the voyage being a "greasy" one.

With the reputation of being a successful whaleman Cash was offered, and accepted, the position of master of the ship *Gideon Howland*, to be gone until April 1850.

By this time Azubah had carried on at home long enough.

She made up her mind to go to sea with her husband and told him: "You have been home less than twenty-six weeks in our eleven years of marriage. I am going with you."

Mrs. Cash lived aboard a whaler from that time until her captain husband retired, and they returned to Cotuit.

Life at sea was hard, but loneliness at home was worse, so Caroline Mayhew accompanied her captain husband on his whaling expeditions. The sailors were always happy when she was aboard, as the captain's language and treatment of them was somewhat tempered by her presence. She spent her time teaching the children their reading and arithmetic, writing letters, keeping a diary, playing the organ which she had brought on ship, and, occasionally, ventured into the galley and made pies, to the delight of the men on board.

When eight men of the ship *Powhatan* came down with small pox they were doctored by Mrs. Mayhew, and all recovered. The crew was so grateful to her that they presented her with their choicest scrimshaw articles, jagging wheels with intricate designs, swifts doweled with coin silver, slender bodkins, and knitting needles inlaid with decorative woods. These gifts are still treasured by the Mayhew descendents.

Captain Charles Grant furnished an added incentive to his crew to watch for whales by offering a silver dollar to anyone sighting one. The captain's wife, who had shipped out with her husband aboard a whaler out of Nantucket, and whose son, George, was born on a tiny South Pacific island, was the first to sight a whale after the reward was offered. Hanging out the family wash on the spanker boom, Mrs. Grant saw a whale surfacing in the distance.

"Blow, Blow, — there she blows," she shouted, clothespins which she was holding in her mouth flying in all directions.

You can imagine the joyful shouting, and scrambling into the whaleboats upon hearing her call.

The captain gladly presented her with a silver dollar.

The town of Falmouth, Massachusetts, with a population of only about 2,000 people during the first half of the nineteenth century, was late in entering the whaling industry. By this time nearly all the whaling grounds had been opened up by Yankee seamen, but it has been estimated that 148 captains put to sea from this small port during this period.

It was a captain's wife from Falmouth, however, who claimed the honor of being the first white woman, as far as is known, to go ashore and spend some time in Japan. An isolated empire, Japan, as late as 1853, had permitted no foreigners on its territory under penalty of death.

Mrs. Cordelia Childs, wife of Captain Peter Childs, accompanied her husband on a whaling expedition into the Pacific and in the year 1845 put into a Japanese port. The people of southern Yego, far distant from the seat of government in Yedo, and with communication being poor and late in arriving, were not appraised, apparently of the government edict. They were friendly and curious when the whaler anchored off shore and a white lady disembarked.

Mrs. Childs spent several days in the little community, and often told, when she returned to Falmouth of the interest and wonder expressed by the inhabitants, how they fingered her clothing, and how carefully they received the material, gadgets and jewelry which the sailors offered in return for much needed fruit, vegetables and fresh water.

The whaling wives coped with life and death almost daily, enduring hardship, loneliness and monotony, but, to a woman, preferred to be with their husbands at sea than alone at home. They sailed from the South seas to the Arctic, from the New England homeport to Japan and China, and, by their presence made the entire world one world and the whaling families and the whaling industry an important part of it.

Ship Uncas – Whaling – Artist unknown. Ship Uncas was built in Falmouth, Mass. 1828; sold to New Bedford 1843. Whaling ground – Pacific. Courtesy Richard A. Bourne Co. Inc.

V   The Perils Of Whaling

The perils of whale fishery were many and would be enough to discourage the faint-hearted. Violent storms, hurricane winds, mountainous waves threatened the ships and boats.

In *Pursuing The Whale* by Captain John A. Cook one such "blow" is described. Captain Cook signed on the schooner *William Martin* of Boston as boatsteerer when a young man. He writes of his first voyage as being uneventful "save for a hurricane which we encountered August 17" ('1879) "which came near being the end of us all. It blew so hard that the schooner just lay on her side, and when the order to cut away the mast was given no man could execute it, so buried under the water was the whole vessel." When the weather moderated they found they had only one boat left, the rudder post sprung, the stern badly strained, the bulwarks all gone, "in fact, almost a total wreck, and in this condition we made for New Bedford."

"Man overboard" was a dreaded cry, for, in storms and gigantic waves, there was little chance of rescuing an unfortunate victim. We find in one of Captain DeBlois' letters: "I ran to the lee quarter and thought I saw a glimpse of the poor fellow, but we could do nothing in the sea that was running," 'The poor fellow' was a young man, twenty-two years old, who had run away from home to seek his fortune whale fishing.

Getting lost from the mother ship while pursuing the whale was among the foremost hazards, as well as being capsized by an angry or wounded whale. A terse notation in Nantucket *Argument Settlers* states: 1820 — "Loss of ship *Essex* in Pacific ocean, November 20, sunk by a whale. Survivors of crew were obliged to resort to cannibalism in order that any might return alive."

The natives on the islands which the whaling ships touched or were stranded were not always friendly, and, in one case, the ship *Twilight* out of New Bedford, was destroyed on the island of Hivaca, but the crew was protected by a resident missionary.

The ships that went into the Arctic were often frozen in for the winter and were constantly in danger of being crushed by the ice. Icebergs accounted for many lost ships and crews, the *Frank* out of Mystic, Connecticut, being one that struck an iceberg and was lost at Desolation Island.

Coast-wise, along the Atlantic seaboard during the Civil War, dozens of Yankee whaling ships were captured and burned, their crews put in irons. The *Shenandoah* accounted for 90% of those destroyed in this manner, "captured and burned by the *Shenandoah*," and "captured and burned by the *Florida;* their crew put in irons."

One finds stark and concise data on the whaleships sent out to seek whales recorded in the Report of the Commissioner of Fish and Fisheries. Here are a few statistics taken at random from the Records during the period 1855-1865:

The *Nantucket,* a ship out of Nantucket on June 4, 1855, Richard C. Gibbs, captain, was driven ashore and lost on Nashawena when homeward bound with 736 barrels of sperm oil, 794 of whale oil. Fortunately, the loss was somewhat allayed by the fact that she had sent home, previous to the disaster, 240 sperm, 320 whale, and 3,000 pounds of bone.

The Bark *Montgomery,* William R. Chapman, captain, Swift and Allen, owners, set out from New Bedford on August 23, 1855 for the Pacific Ocean. On November 19, 1856 the third mate and boat's crew were lost, fast to a whale.

The *Mount Vernon,* a ship, E. F. Nye, captain, David R. Greene & Company, owners, set out for the North Pacific on

September 1, 1855, was stove by ice and sunk in Ochotsk on June 15, 1856.

Vigilant, a bark, Joseph McCleave the captain, W. and G. D. Watkins, owners, set out from New Bedford for the Pacific November 16, 1855 and returned May 28, 1859 having lost the third mate and four men by running a loose whale while fast to another and the boat upsetting.

The *Superior,* a bark out of New Bedford, Richard D. Wood, captain, James B. Wood & Company owners, sailed for the Pacific June 24, 1857 and was burned by natives of the Solomon Islands; all but six of the crew were massacred in September 1860.

In April 1857 the schooner *E. Nickerson,* John Pettengill captain, Samuel Soper owner, set out from Provincetown for the North Atlantic and became a missing vessel. The captain had his wife and two children with him.

The bark *Clara Bell,* out of Mattapoisett, Timothy Fisher captain, R. L. Barstow owner, sailed for the Pacific Ocean on June 24, 1858. A boat's crew was lost in December 1863 while fast to a whale.

On October 19, 1859 the bark *Newark,* Nathan Smith captain, C. Hitch & Son owners, set out from New Bedford for the Indian Ocean. It was lost on Sandal Wood Island (Malay Archipelago) April 7, 1863. Its crew was in boats 9 days and 10 nights with but little bread and water.

The *Roscoe,* a bark out of New Bedford, Will H. Almy captain, Loum Snow owner or agent, set out for the Pacific November 1859. The captain and seven men (part of two boats' crews) were killed by a whale.

The *Syren Queen,* a ship out of Fairhaven, C. R. Chapel captain, Gibbs & Jenney owners, set out for Davis Strait on June 13, 1860; lost five men by scurvy on the expedition.

A Fairhaven brig, *Pavilion,* its captain Ichabod Handy, owners Damon & Judd, set out for Hudson Bay June 15, 1863, and was lost in Hudson Bay, crushed by ice. Seven men were lost, the survivors suffered severely from cold and exposure.

The *James Maury,* a ship out of New Bedford, S. L. Gray, captain, C. R. Tucker & Co. owner, set out on June 1, 1864 for the North Pacific. Captain Gray died at Guam on May 24, 1865. The ship was captured by the *Shenandoah* in Behring Strait in

June 1865 and was bonded because Captain Gray's wife was on board.

The *Hector,* out of New Bedford, captained by Amos A. Chase, owner William Rotch, sent home 260 barrels of sperm oil, 140 whale oil and 1,850 pounds of bone before she was captured and burned by the rebel *Shenandoah* at Ascension in 1865.

The *Pacific,* a bark out of Sag Harbor, New York, — French, captain, owners H & S French, left port August 14, 1865, was lost at Behring's Island on July 30, 1866. The third mate and five men arrived at Hakodadi, after being two months in an open boat.

These brief entries, concise and tragic, read like notes for adventure stories, and carry all the misery, hardship, suffering and despair endured in pursuing the whale.

Belaying Pin – a removable pin in the rail of a ship, around which ropes can be fastened.

Belaying Pins – used to secure rope – Courtesy Heritage Plantation of Sandwich/TFA

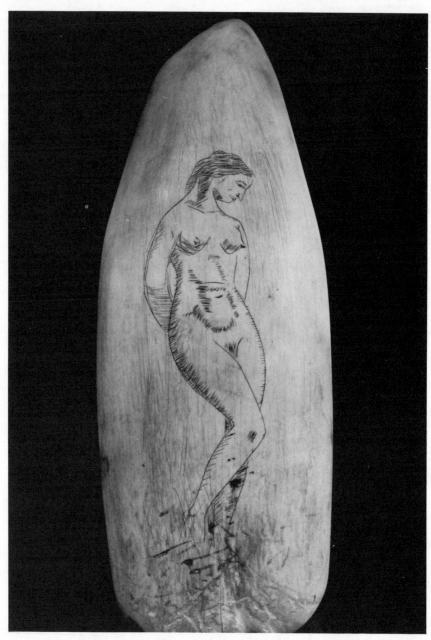

Nude – Scrimshaw design on Sperm tooth. Author's Collection.

VI   Explorers in the South Pacific

Excerpt from Nantucket *Argument Settlers*

1791 — The first Nantucket whaleship to sail around Cape Horn
entered the Pacific Ocean this year. She was the ship *Beaver,*
captain Paul Worth, carrying a crew of seventeen men, and
manning five boats. Her voyage lasted seventeen months. Six
other Nantucket whaleships entered the South Pacific this
same year.

Many Pacific islands and reefs bear the names of their dis-
coverers, — captains and merchants from Nantucket and New
Bedford. In 1808 Mayhew Folger, captain of the *Topaz* out of
Nantucket, happened upon uncharted Pitcairn Island where
Fletcher Christian and his fellow mutineers took refuge in 1789.
Another Nantucket captain, Timothy Folger, cousin of Benjamin
Franklin, was the first to map the Gulf Stream. And "Sunset Lon-
gitude" was discovered by Owen C. Spooner of Nantucket while
on the ship *Atlantic,* December 16, 1840.

Yankee whalemen were the foremost authorities on Pacific
and South Pacific aborigines, — their habitat and culture, — but
their accounts of these native peoples and their contacts with them
seem to have been carefully censored; little was revealed by word
of mouth and scarcely anything was written. It is known, however,
that life on most of these isles was very pleasant; some whalers
were so enamoured with the islands and their inhabitants that they
jumped ship and spent the rest of their days in tropical bliss.

Friendly natives welcomed the whalemen for purposes of bar-
ter, anxious to trade fresh water, fruits and vegetables and native
wood for tools, implements, clothing and jewelry. Upon sighting
a ship they boarded their native canoes and swarmed onto the
ships in hordes. Some captains and mates tried to keep the ship
off-limits for the natives (young women were enticing and willing,
and the men sometimes had plans to try to capture the ship), but
it was almost impossible to keep them off the vessel.

In Melville's picturesque account of a lay-over in Resolution Bay by the *Acushnet* in 1842 we read: "We had approached within a mile and a half perhaps of the foot of the bay when some of the islanders — who had managed to scramble aboard directed our attention to a singular commotion in the water ahead — . At first I imagined it to be produced by a shoal of fish — but our savage friends assured us that it was caused by a shoal of "Whinhenies" (Young Girls) — coming off shore to welcome us — some distance from the beach — they boarded us at every quarter, many seizing hold of the chain plates and springing into the chains. Others, at the peril of being run over — catching at the bob stay and wreathing their slender forms about the ropes, hung suspended in the air. All of them at length succeeded in getting up the ship's sides where they clung, dripping with brine and glowing from the bath, their jet black tresses streaming over their shoulders and half enveloping their otherwise naked forms —."

Nelson C. Haley, harpooner on the *Charles W. Morgan,* wrote in his journal: "Sat. Jan. 29, 1845. P.M. fine weather. Byron's Island in sight and about 40 or 50 canoes alongside with 4 or 5 natives in each one. There was some of the Ladies came to be our wives. Land in sight off both beams."

Some captains and mates who expected to get back to the area at some future date went through mock wedding ceremonies with the alluring satin-skinned native girls; (few, if any, entered into bigamous marriages by engaging in Christian ceremonies), thus maintaining households in the balmy southern climes and on the stark New England coast.

Most of the sailors lived with the island girls without benefit of any ceremony. The young women entered into these relationships casually and willingly as it was considered an honor to be the mistress of a Yankee whaleman; indeed, the family of such a young woman merited the esteem of other islanders when this situation existed.

Thus, the pursuance of the sperm whale in the South Pacific had more far reaching results than the accruement of barrels of oil and bundles of bone.

VII The Art of Scrimshaw

Scrimshaw consists of incising ivory or bone with intricate designs or patterns into which color is rubbed to accentuate highlights and shading. It was the art of the whalemen only, carried on in the long weary days of waiting for the appearance of a whale. More recently other handcrafts fashioned by whalemen have also been included in the term "scrimshaw".

No one knows precisely where the word "scrimshaw" originated. Since seamen were notoriously poor spellers and wrote things as they sounded, we find "squimshon", "Scrimshone", "scrimshorn", and "skrimshand" in journals and logs of the whalemen. There is a Dutch word "skrimshander", meaning "idle fellow" or "one who fritters the time away", from which "scrimshaw" seems a likely derivative.

A log entry of one such whaler records: "This is terribly slow traveling, ship has made thirty-nine miles of nothing since yesterday. All hands skrimshandering. So ends this very long day."

Using whatever tools were at hand on board ship scrimshandering furnished diversion and entertainment for idle hands and minds. One may reasonably assume that it was our first experiment in "occupational therapy". Such handwork was a refuge for homesick whalemen bored with the monotony of waiting for a "Blow, blo-o-ow, — there she blows" when the watch, high in the rigging, spotted a whale.

Scrimshaw is known as the only indigenous American folk art, other than that of the American Indian. Incorporating, in various degrees, artistic sense, dexterity, powers of observation and materials at hand, each piece was an "original". It might display exceptional talent, or the crude and painstaking work of an inept and lovesick sailor. A typical inscription reads: — "When This You See/Remember Me/Though Many Miles/We Distant Be." Surrounded by a wreath of interwoven roses, forget-me-nots and trailing vines, a busk decorated thus furnished many happy hours for a lonely lad and was a fitting valentine for his beloved.

Each scrimshander was allotted his share of teeth, whalebone and baleen scraps to decorate as he pleased and to dispose of as he wished. It has been estimated that some sixty varieties of articles were products of the handcraft of the whalemen. These decorated pieces of ivory and bone were not for sale, but were souvenirs, — mementoes to take back home to wives, mothers, sweethearts, children and friends. Many were pictorial records of their daily lives and encounters; others were strictly fantasies. Knowing that they had plenty of time and with nothing else to occupy their minds, the seamen could give vent to stark realism, nostalgia, or imagination, while they dreamed of home.

Articles fashioned by the scrimshander fall into four broad categories, — something useful, decorative, ornamental, or a toy.

Useful articles include almost every tool and piece of equipment used on a ship, — blocks, belaying pins, fids (used in splicing rope), bodkins (needles of various sizes), stamps for log books, carpenters' tools, rulers, ditty boxes; for the household, — sewing boxes, needles, spools, writing desks and boxes, picture frames, swifts, rolling pins, clothes pins, jagging wheels (pie crimpers), napkin rings, spoolers, busks (stays for women's corsets), hair pins. Jewelry included rings, earrings, brooches, lockets, bracelets, stick pins, cuff links, hair combs.

Scrimshawed teeth were strictly ornamental, as were models of ships, whaleboats, carved whales and seals.

A great deal of thought and ingenuity went into playthings, where we find dolls, doll houses and furniture, dominoes, checkers, cribbage boards, chess men, sleds, tops, pen holders, and many of the adult artifacts in miniature.

Herman Melville sailed on his whaling voyage on the bark *Acushnet* in 1841, and scrimshaw was, even then, a widespread art. He wrote: "Throughout the Pacific, and also in Nantucket and New Bedford and Sag Harbor, you will come across lively sketches of whales and whaling scenes graven by the fishermen themselves on sperm teeth, or ladies' busks wrought out of the right whalebone, or other like scrimshander articles, as the whale-men call the numerous little ingenious contrivances they elaborately carve out of the rough material in their hours of leisure."

From *Bertha Goes Whaling* by Mrs. Bertha Hamblin Boyce in which she recounts her experiences when a child aboard the bark *Islander*, captained by her father, John C. Hamblin, we find this interesting reference to scrimshaw: "Sometimes days went by without sighting a whale. This was rather dull for the sailors, so they spent their time making things out of whalebone, — are called scrimshaw. I have two beautiful boxes made of whalebone. My father was a 33rd degree Mason and one design was a Masonic emblem. They also made India ink pictures on large whales' teeth. I also have what is called a swift for winding yarn. It is adjustable so you can wind a large or small skein. They made a fork of whale bone with a wheel on one end which they called a gadging wheel used to crimp pies. My mother used one of these. She must have crimped hundreds of pies for her big family and many guests. She didn't have time to make cookies (cut out), so she made what she called 'hard gingerbread'. The top was ornamented with the wheel."

Whalebone Vase – rare scrimshaw vase formed from mounting a whale's tooth with tip down on turned ivory with baleen decoration. Top has scroll cutting. Author's Collection.

37

Busks – Scrimshawed whalebone stays for a lady's bodice. Author's Collection.

VIII Popular Scrimshaw Articles
The Busk

The first article that a scrimshander etched was also the most personal. Intended as a stay in the front of a woman's bodice, or corset, the busk was about twelve inches long and two inches wide, with a thickness of one eighth to one fourth inch. It was made of 'pan bone', the lower jaw of a sperm whale, or of baleen, the plates in the mouth of the right whale. Its size often depended on the material available, and the measurements of its intended recipient.

A flat surface, fairly easy to inscribe when green, even with a jack knife, the sailor's thoughts and longings were crowded onto these scraps of bone.

'Hidden next to her heart', the sentiment expressed could be for her, and her alone, and was portrayed by hearts entwined with flowers and vines; romantic pictures and verses interspersed with geometric designs including circles, diamonds, triangles, stars, loops and teardrops.

A weeping willow was sometimes traced beside which drooped a grieving female figure to impart loneliness and homesickenss. Nostalgia and thoughts of home were also expressed by likenesses of the home cottage, familiar landmarks and seascapes.

Patriotism had its place, oftentimes, with waving American flags and likenesses of popular political figures. Only a few reflected the whaleman's occupation, i.e. whaleships, whaleboats and whales.

The verses used were often original, usually using such words as 'remember', 'love', 'wait', 'return', 'home'. Four of the most often used, authors unknown, were as follows:

"Rest on the bossum of the fair
And softly whisper Peace
Bid every sorrow, every care
And dark foreboding cease."

"Accept dear Girl this busk from me
Carved by my humble hand
I took it from a Sperm Whale's jaw
One thousand miles from land."

"This bone once in a spermwhale's jaw did rest
Now 'tis intended for a woman's brest.
This, my love, I do intend
For you to wear and not to lend."

"In many a gale
Has been the whale
  In which this bone did rest.
His time is past
His bone at last
  Must now support thy breast."

An unusual verse (to find in a sailor's artwork), finely etched in script and almost indecipherable on the blackened baleen busk:

"Full many a gem of purest ray serene
The dark unfathomed caves of ocean bear,
Full many a flower is born to blush unseen
And waste its sweetness on the desert air."
(from Gray's *Elegy Written In A Country Churchyard*.)

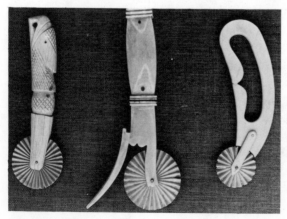

Jagging Wheels – intricately carved and decorated whale ivory pie crust or cookie cutters. Courtesy Richard A. Bourne Co. Inc.

Jagging Wheels

Every mother or wife expected a jagging wheel, or pie crust crimper, from her returning whaleman. Although more difficult to fashion, requiring exacting and painstaking work, they were a popular item for scrimshanders to make and are found in every scrimshaw collection.

The jagging wheel consisted of a handle, or shank, on one end of which was a revolving wheel, on the other end may, or may not, have been a two or three-tined fork. They were used to cut and crimp the edges of pies, to cut strips for the tops of open pies, and as cookie cutters. The fork was used to make perforations in top crusts to allow steam to escape, for artistic decoration, and to test the 'doneness' of the contents of the pie.

Carved from a single piece of ivory or bone, the wheel itself was more or less standard, the difference being in the design of the fluted edges. The ingenuity and dexterity of the artist became apparent in the handles. Their designs were legion.

Overall, jagging wheels were about six to eight inches long, and were executed in the forms of human figures, birds, animals, butterflies, fish, flowers and initials. There were cut-outs, inlays of baleen, ebony and mother-of-pearl. Buffed and polished they were a beautiful work of art and was valued highly by the woman favored to receive it.

Many a homesick lad dreamed of the apple, blueberry or pumpkin pie his mother would make when he returned home while he labored over a pie crimper to decorate them.

This brings to mind a story told and re-told in New Bedford circles. It was the custom, during the whaling years in New Bedford, to hold church suppers or socials, when the sailors returned to homeport. The women brought their most delectable and outstanding culinary efforts, the affair often ending in a pie contest. A prize was given to the best decorated and most delicious pie.

At one such social the elderly mother of a recently returned sailor was awarded the prize and congratulated by the judges.

"That was a delicious pie and beautifully trimmed. Did Joe bring you a new pie crimper?"

She replied, "Land sakes, I didn't use no pie crimper on that pie. I used my false teeth."

Swifts

The swift, or yarn winder, was another favorite item intended for wife, mother or sweetheart. Due to the necessity for exact measurements and the intricacies of its performance, a man had to be practically a mechanical genius to produce this article. It is considered in the scrimshaw category mainly because it was an artistic work executed in the whaleman's 'idle hours'.

Similar to a small clothes reel, the swift was made of dozens of small pieces of bone, — sliced, trimmed, measured, polished and assembled. These pieces were then carefully joined by means of knots or by pegs, so that the reel could be raised or lowered on its axis spoke, not unlike opening and closing an umbrella. A thumb screw, fitting on the lower sleeve, secured the reel in the desired position, and another attached the winder to the table.

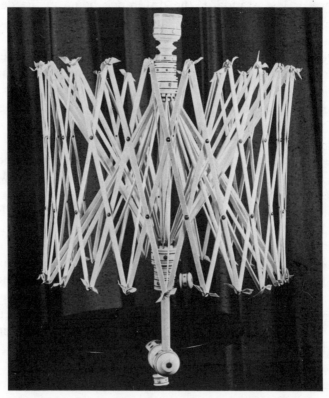

Swift – delicately carved and meticulously assembled whalebone yarn winder. Author's Collection.

When open, the swifts measured about fifteen inches across and five to eight inches high; the axis spoke being fifteen to twenty inches. The top of the axis spoke often ended in a pin cushion or a bowl in which to place an unfinished ball of yarn. The base was decorated by carved figures, or inlaid with a design of ebony, baleen, mother-of-pearl, or abalone shell.

Because of the fragile material and intricacy of design swifts had a high rate of mortality, and a complete one in good working order is eagerly sought by present day collectors.

Sewing Boxes

Sewing boxes were given and received with extreme pride. Fashioned for wife or sweetheart, her name or initials were often inlaid on the top or front center, and outfitted with the loved one's particular talents and needs in mind.

Both utilitarian and decorative, sewing boxes were made of native wood inlaid in various designs with ivory or ebony, or were carved entirely of ivory. They were beautiful examples of craftmanship, containing one or more drawers, and outfitted with every imaginable sewing necessity, ivory thimbles, needles, darning egg, spools and winders for thread and silk, sewing birds, thumb screws and clamps for anchoring cloth to a table, pin cushions, ivory cutouts for crewel designs and embroidery patterns. Some of the larger boxes have even been equipped with knitting needles and crochet hooks of varying sizes, all made of ivory.

Often a little girl's first sewing box was presented to her by a sailor father on his return from a whaling expedition.

The sailor's ditty box, made of baleen and decorated with scenes and images which he saw or dreamed of, was a variety of sewing box. It contained not only his small personal effects but small bodkins and needles for mending and repairing clothing and canvas.

In this category may also be found work boxes, trinket and jewelry boxes, thread stands and spoolers. The latter were tiered stands with a drawer or two, made of mahogany or teakwood with a design or the recipient's name inlaid with ivory, baleen or mother-of-pearl, on the front. The pegs for holding the spools of thread were of ivory and arranged for easy viewing and selecting.

Sewing Box – mahogany with pine and sub-woods – three drawers inlaid with Whale ivory hearts and arrows, diamonds and stars while top features stars, crescent moons, diamonds and a large knob on which may have been mounted a swift. Courtesy Richard A. Bourne Co. Inc.

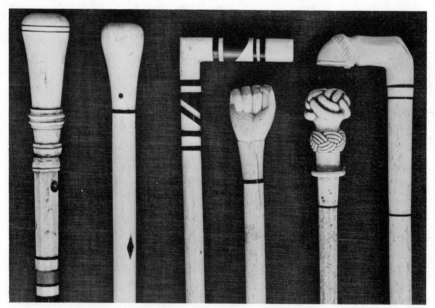

Canes – Beautifully carved walking sticks, variously inlaid with baleen, abalone shell, mahogany and ebony. Courtesy Richard A. Bourne Co. Inc.

44

Canes

Every collector of canes will want several examples of scrimshaw in his collection, and every collector of scrimshaw will include canes. In the early nineteenth century a man's affluence was often judged by the length and amount of decoration of his walking stick.

Scrimshaw canes or walking sticks were popular subjects and comparatively easy to make. Constructed from a single piece of jaw bone they measured about three feet long and averaged from one to two inches in diameter, allowing for carving and final rubbing down. The variety of knobs and their degree of execution, the cut-outs, inlays and carvings on the shafts, showed the interests and abilities of the artist. These included the "Friendship Hand", rope-carved knob, round, oval and fluted knobs, a snake or vine winding up the shaft. Horizontal handles were fashioned in the shape of a whale, a running fox or dog, or a woman's bent knee.

Of these the "Friendship Hand" was most frequently used. It is found in almost every scrimshaw category and carries a message which can be understood. The "Friendship Hand" is a clenched fist, sometimes carved with a cuff at the wrist, and signifies "good-will", "peace", "friendliness".

An interesting account in the *Village Advertiser*, a weekly newspaper published in Centerville, Massachusetts, on February 9, 1972, tells of a scrimshawed whalebone cane awarded to the oldest resident of Osterville.

The article relates that Mr. William Blount, a resident of Osterville at the time of his death in 1871, was born in London, England, and served as a seaman on the British frigate, *Guerriere*. He was taken prisoner aboard the *U.S. Constitution* during the famous encounter between the two ships.

Mr. Blount became a naturalized citizen in 1844 and settled in Osterville. Here he made wooden bungs for whale oil barrels, transporting them by ox cart to Woods Hole. The ivory walking stick was his prized possession and he left it by will to be handed down to the oldest resident of Osterville. Twenty men and women have held the cane since that time. The present holder is Mrs. Frank Allen.

Bodkins

There was a variety of tools in the spike and needle category. The larger ones were called fids and spikes. Large, stiletto-type instruments, they were used when splicing and working rope and heavy cord. Being strictly utilitarian they offered little incentive for artistry or ingenuity.

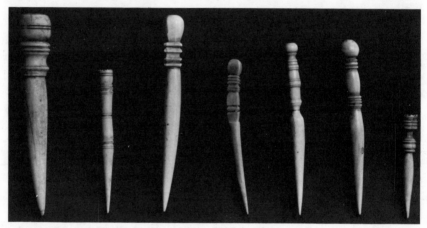

Bodkins – whale bone needles, Courtesy Heritage Plantation of Sandwich/TFA

Bodkins, on the other hand, were small needles used for taping, sewing, weaving and mat-making. Carved from a solid piece of bone, remnants of slab, teeth, or jawbone, their shafts measured from three to five inches. They were straight or curved like a scimitar and tapered to slender points.

Slender and delicate, some bodkins had eyes for threading; most, however, had small butts at their bases which could be clasped between thumb and forefinger, making it easy to work holes and push yarn and thread through them.

These sewing needles were graceful and delicate tools, often fashioned with intricate carving and exquisite inlay of contrasting materials, — mahogany, teak, mother-of-pearl and abalone. To those scrimshanders with genuine artistic talent they offered fulfillment and joy-of accomplishment.

Comparatively small and slender, bodkins have been lost or broken through the intervening years and, when found, make a choice addition to a scrimshaw collection.

Doll Bed – Courtesy Heritage Plantation of Sandwich/TFA

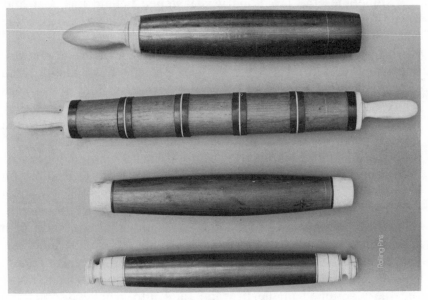

Rolling Pins – Courtesy Heritage Plantation of Sandwich/TFA.

47

IX Sperm Teeth

The bulk of all scrimshaw was made from the teeth of the sperm whale (ivory). Only sperms have teeth, and they, only on their lower jaws.

Sperm whales were vigorously pursued all over the world by our Yankee whalers. They were most highly prized for two reasons, they produced by far the better oil, and, at times, a valuable substance, called 'ambergris', was found in their intestines. The fact that Sperms came equipped with teeth was an added dividend.

According to an account in *The Cruise Of The Cachalot* by Frank Bullen, First Mate, "The lower jaw of this whale measured exactly nineteen feet in length from the opening of the mouth, or, say the last of the teeth, to the point, and carried twenty-eight teeth on each side. For the time it was hauled aft out of the way, and secured to the lash-rail."

Sometimes the jaw bone was fastened behind the boat and towed for a period of time, then hauled on deck and dried, after which it was a fairly easy matter to remove the teeth.

Mate Bullen continues: "After every sign of the operations had been cleared away, the jaw was brought out and the teeth extracted with a small tackle. They were set solidly into a hard white gum, which had to be cut away all around them before they would come out. When cleaned of the gum, they were headed up in a small barrel of brine. The great jaw-pans were sawn off, and placed at the disposal of anybody who wanted pieces of 'scrimshaw', or carved work. This is a very favorite pastime on board whalers, — '. But our carpenter was a famous workman at 'scrimshaw', and he started half a dozen walking-sticks forthwith. A favorite design is to carve the bone into the similitude of a rope, with 'worming' of smaller lines along its lays. A handle is carved out of a whale's tooth, and insets of baleen, silver, or ebony, give variety and finish. The tools used are the roughest. Some old files, softened in the fire and filed into grooves, something like saw-teeth, are most used; but old knives, sail-needles, and chisels are pressed into service. The work turned out would, in many cases, take a very high place in an exhibition of turnery, though never a lathe was near it. Of course a long time is taken over it, especially the polishing, which is done with oil and whiting, if it can be got — powdered pumice if it cannot."

When "green", or recently harvested, the teeth were not difficult to inscribe. They acquired their brittleness and hardness with exposure to air. The surfaces were, however, rigid and rough, and required a great deal of smoothing and polishing before they could be etched. Files and grindstones, which were found on every sea-going vessel to keep an edge on whaling instruments and bodkins needle-sharp, were used. A final smoothing with shark skin was necessary before polishing with wood ash from under the blubber pot. At this point elbow grease and patience made the difference between a fairly respectable piece and a true work of art. The more vigor used in rubbing the surface, the higher the luster.

To work the graphics the whalemen used what they had at hand. Using a jack knife or a sail needle embedded in a wooden handle the drawings could be etched finely or deeply to give dimension and shading. Nails could be filed to a fine point for outlines, and gouges or small chisels used to countersink inlay work. Whenever possible the natural markings were worked into the design of a tooth, giving a harmonious blending of material and art.

Color was produced by rubbing or tracing into the cut surfaces India ink, lamp black, soot from under the try-pots, or logwood, — black being the principal color since it was more readily available. Tobacco juice gave a mellow sepia; the juice of berries and certain plants found on tropical islands colored some of the work.

Most outlines were free hand, but, sometimes, a sailor would want to record something from the fashion world. At such times a page from a Godey book, brought on board at the beginning of the voyage for perusal and reading, was pasted on the tooth and an outline made by a series of small punctures.

One tooth, with rare humor, depicts on one side a New England matron, in typical Victorian gown, voluminous and bustled; on the other, a scantily-clad South Sea native girl, with the inscription: "Our wives and sweethearts, may they never meet."

X   Famous Teeth

The teeth most prized are those inscribed with dates, names of specific vessels, captains, artists, and scenes of identifiable ports, cities and shorelines.

Collectors' items of great interest and rare value include several teeth decorated by a seaman named Frederick Myrick. These were the first signed and dated teeth of which there is any record. What makes them distinct and choice is the fact that they describe, pictorially, various whaling episodes with which the artist was familiar, and adds the name of the ship, of the captain, and his own; also, the date of the voyage — *Susan* 1826 — 1830 — the ship's first voyage around the Horn.

One of these teeth was in a Cape Cod marine auction recently. After much spirited bidding it was awarded to the ecstatic purchaser for $11,000.00.

Mr. Bourne, the auctioneer, described it in this manner: The most important piece of scrimshaw ever offered by this firm and most certainly the ultimate piece in any collection of the whalers' folk art. This rare example is, to the best of our knowledge, the nineth one so far discovered. It is also the only one of which we are aware which is mounted in South American silver. One can readily speculate as to how the tooth came to be so mounted, as whale ships frequently touched the South American coast at Chile for replenishment of supplies and rest before the long voyage home.

The tooth is engraved overall with the ship with two of her boats off her bow attacking whales. A banner over the ship reads "The *Susan* boiling and killing sperm whales." The other side shows the *Susan* cutting into a whale while three of her boats attack a pod of whales off her bow. A banner over the ship reads "The *Susan* on the coast of Japan." On the narrow side of the tooth are inscribed the words "Ship *Susan* of Nantucket/Frederick Swain/Master." Around the tip of the tooth are engraved crossed American flags and an anchor and the following words "Engraved by Fred Myrick on board of the *Susan* February the 23d 1829."

The tooth is also engraved with an American eagle holding a banner which reads "E PLURIBUS UNUM".

Of the eight other *Susan's* teeth that are known all are in either museums or private collections, and this is the first time, to our knowledge, that one has ever been offered at public auction."

In 1955 Mr. Everett N. Crosby of Nantucket wrote a monograph in which he describes, with illustrations, the etchings on each of seven teeth which he had acquired. Titled *Susan's Teeth* the book has also joined the ranks of rare and treasured memorabilia. A bibliophile recently paid $400.00 for a copy and considered it a bargain.

A rare, one-of-a-kind scrimshawed whale's tooth is engraved and colored with a full-figure portrait of the female pirate captain, Fanny Campbell, on one side; on the other the portrait of an American brig, also in color.

A book *Fanny Campbell* by Lieutenant Murray, published in Baltimore in 1845, tells the story of the famous Fanny Campbell who dressed as a man, called herself Captain Channing, and sailed her ship to Cuba where she rescued her lover from a Cuban prison. On her return Captain Channing captured a British armed sloop and put the crew in irons. Her crew never knew she was not a man.

Fanny's portrait on the whale's tooth is an exact copy of the frontispiece of the book.

The *Ann Alexander,* out of New Bedford in June 1850, its captain John Scott DeBlois, was one of three ships known to have been rammed and sunk by a whale, (the other two — *Essex* out of Nantucket in 1818, and the *Kathleen,* of New Bedford in 1902).

Pained and angered when struck by a harpoon, a bull whale rushed two whaleboats, one after the other, seizing each in his gigantic jaws and smashing them to pieces, scattering the occupants of the boats into the water. Rescued by a third boat commandeered by the captain, the crew returned to the *Ann Alexander* and proceeded to attack the monster from her deck.

Still infuriated, the whale rushed the ship at a speed of fifteen knots and struck a terrific blow two feet from the keel and just abreast of the foremast. This opened a huge hole in the ship's

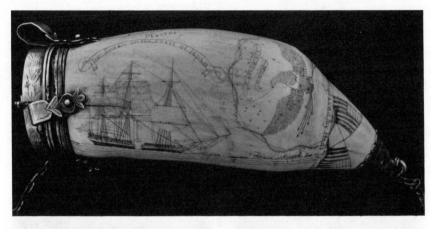

Susan's Tooth – "Engraved by Fred Myrick on board of the Susan February the 23d 1829". Scrimshawed teeth with a date are very important. Courtesy Richard A. Bourne Co. Inc.

bottom through which the water started to pour. As soon as the extent of the damage was realized Captain DeBlois ordered the crew into the remaining whaleboats. With chronometer, sextant, and charts in his arms the captain was the last man to leave the ship.

Escaping with only three gallons of water and twenty pounds of sodden bread (all that they had been able to rescue) the *Ann Alexander's* captain and crew were extremely fortunate to be picked up two days later, on August 22, 1850, by the *Nantucket,* out of Nantucket, Richard C. Gibbs, her captain.

By a strange quirk of fate, Captain Jernegon, of the *Rebecca Simms*, raised this same whale about five months later, captured and killed him. He seemed old and tired with wooden splinters deeply imbedded in his head, and several of the *Ann Alexander's* irons fast in his carcass. A scrimshander etched some of the teeth with appropriate designs and presented them to Captain DeBlois.

Scrimshaw executed on this ill -fated ship is extremely rare and exceedingly valuable.

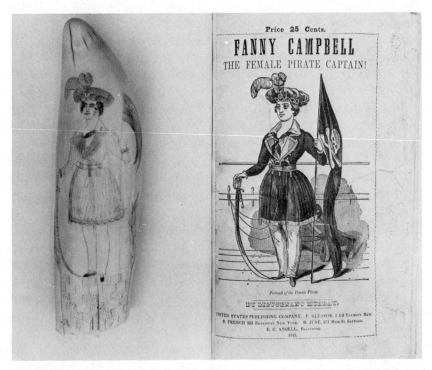

Fanny Campbell – rare scrimshawed whale's tooth, engraved and colored full figured portrait of Fanny Campbell, female pirate captain; also picture of book by "Lieutenant Murray" who wrote the story of Fanny Campbell. These two pieces are now in the Heritage Plantation Scrimshaw Exhibit.

XI Scrimshaw Collectors

Most collectors of scrimshaw are, or were, lovers of the sea. President John F. Kennedy was a dedicated collector of whales' teeth, having in his collection, at the time of his death, thirty-four etched whales' teeth and three decorated walrus tusks. During his presidency they were all displayed in his office in the White House. They are now on exhibition in the Kennedy Library in Cambridge, Massachusetts.

Knowing his love of the sea Mrs. Kennedy gave her husband, in 1960, a whale's tooth on which was traced an American ship under full sail. Intensely interested in marine and historical Americana, all of the pieces which Mr. Kennedy selected thereafter were pictures of sailing ships, American naval vessels, encounters with whales, or portraits of historical figures, including George Washington, Abraham Lincoln, Alexander, Ulysses S. Grant, or pictures of historical landmarks, — Independence Hall, Bunker Hill Monument.

Up until the time that it became known that President Kennedy was a scrimshaw collector the interest in these articles had centered chiefly in nautical and historical societies on the New York and New England sea coast. Shortly after 1960 prices started to rise drastically and every antique dealer was scouring coastal towns and even inland areas for the 'folk art' of the American scrimshander'.

In 1962 Jacqueline Kennedy commissioned Milton Delano, one of the few present day creative scrimshaw artists, to inscribe the Presidential Seal on a whale's tooth. Aware of Mr. Kennedy's keen interest in both whaling and history, Mr. Delano chose a huge nine and one-half inch bull whale's tooth, brought back to

New Bedford in 1818 from a whaling expedition, for this important assignment.

Etched, colored and polished, this beautiful work of art was mounted on a piece of walnut panelling taken from the captain's cabin of the whaling bark "Sunbeam".

Presented to her husband by Mrs. Kennedy at Christmas of that year, the whale's tooth, inscribed with the Seal of the President of the United States, held the place of honor on President Kennedy's desk. In the evening of November 24, 1963 it was placed in the President's coffin by the First Lady as a last loving tribute to her husband.

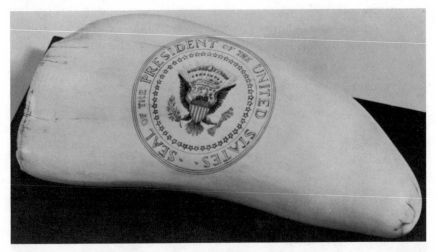

Whale's Tooth with Presidential Seal – Photograph of the whale's tooth, beautifully and meticulously inscribed with the Presidential Seal by Milton Delano, which was placed in President Kennedy's casket the night before his funeral by the First Lady. Photograph: Courtesy of Standard-Times.

Admiral Donald MacMillan spent many years in the Arctic and collected valuable and informative material concerning the area and the people who inhabited it.

He was an enthusiastic collector of ivory, particularly that carved and decorated by the Eskimos; also, scrimshaw which included etchings on walrus tusks and whales' teeth. During his lifetime these artifacts were on display in the Historical Society building in Provincetown, Massachusetts.

Two outstanding whales' teeth in the Admirals's collection were historical in subject and beautifully etched and colored. One portrays John Paul Jones being invested with the Order of Military Merit; the other, "Nomination of Washington As Commander-In-Chief Of The Continental Army".

A few choice pieces are in private collections, but the bulk of Admiral MacMillan's scrimshaw collection, along with other memorabilia of his expeditions, was bequeathed, and now resides, at Bowdoin College, his Alma Mater.

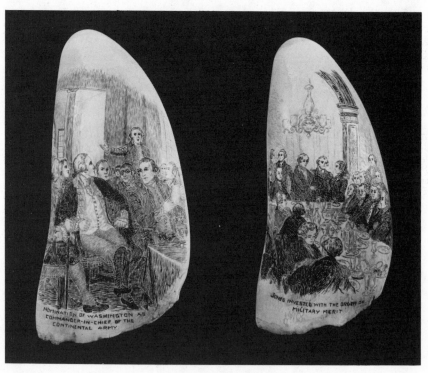

Sperm Teeth With Historic Scenes – originally in MacMillan Collection. Author's Collection.

XII   Whaling Ports and Museums

From the time of her settlement New England was oriented to the sea. Navigation and harvesting the products of the sea were important to her livelihood. Not only did the inhabitants procure food from the ocean but, via the ocean, were connected to other countries and their products.

In the early days roads were little more than foot-paths, and traveling and transporting over them a slow and laborious process. The sea gave a quicker and easier means of communication and exchange with the outside world. It has been said that New England sailors and their families were more familiar with the merchants and peoples of Hong Kong, Singapore, Bombay, London, Paris, Naples and Lisbon than they were with their near-by neighbors in land-locked towns.

As foreign trade and the whaling industry increased, deep and protected harbors were necessary to accommodate the larger vessels. Seaports became the industrial centers and around them grew the resulting concentration of allied businesses and population.

The noisy, thriving whaling ports of Nantucket, New Bedford, Salem, Mystic, Cold Spring Harbor and Sag Harbor are quiet now but historical societies and interested groups have elected to build or establish museums to preserve and display the artifacts and memorabilia of this exciting period in our country's development. We owe them a great deal of gratitude for thus giving us the opportunity to add to our knowledge and understanding of our nation's nautical heritage and to live, vicariously, in the whaling era for a few hours.

Nantucket Island

Situated thirty miles off the New England coast Nantucket Island was dependent upon its own resources for survival and discovered early the necessity of harvesting the products of the sea for commercial exchange with the mainland and other countries. When the first whale was killed and the possibilities of its oil products realized, the whaling industry and ships to transport them became the principal source of Nantucket's income.

Driven out of Massachusetts by a law that forbade the sheltering of Quakers, Thomas Macy purchased Nantucket Island "sachem rights" from the chief of the Natick Indians for thirty pounds and two beaver hats, "one for me and one for my wife." James Forrett, agent for William, the Earl of Sterling, deeded England's interests to Macy and his son in 1641.

Other families with similar beliefs soon joined the Macys and a colony was established. Although these men, the Coffins, the Starbucks, the Folgers, Chases, Husseys, Colemans, and Gardners were not fishermen, the sandy soil and the isolation of the Island made some sort of seafaring necessary. The numerous whales within striking distance and the importance of oil to the mainland made whaling, first off shore and later in distant waters, the obvious industry for Nantucketers.

In 1843 Nantucket owned eighty-eight ships, its greatest number. The decline of ship building and the whaling industry on the Island was due, in part, to a great fire in 1846, but, more drastically, to its harbor not being able to accommodate the larger whaling vessels necessary for the long and more distant expeditions.

Whale fishing voyages did continue to a lesser extent until 1868 when the last whaling vessel owned at Nantucket sailed. It was the bark *R. L. Barstow*.

From the time of the decline of whale fishery as a business summer visitors and tourism became the chief source of the Island's income. Stepping onto the wharf, after a two hour sea voyage, is like stepping into the 18th and 19th centuries. Nantucket Island is, itself, a museum. The beautiful homes of the whaling ships' captains and of the 19th century industrial captains, the Oldest House, Christian Houses, Peter Folger — Hadwen House — Sadler Memorial and the Whaling Museum, all maintained by the Nantucket Historical Association, are impressive memorials to the important whaling industry.

Excerpt from the 1937 Nantucket *Argument Settlers*:

1865 — *Bark Islander,* captain William Cash, while in Pacific Ocean this year, captured a sperm whale 87 feet long, 36 feet in circumference and weighing about 200 tons, yielding 110 barrels of oil. The jaw measured 17 feet in length and was brought to Nantucket, now being a part of the Historical Society's collection.

Although some records have been lost or destroyed by fire, Nantucketers have saved many artifacts of its whaling days and has a good-sized scrimshaw collection as well as whaling gear and implements in its Whaling Musuem. The Museum is open from 10-5 every day, from mid-June to mid-October.

New Bedford

As whaleships became of too great tonnage to be accommodated in Nantucket's harbor, New Bedford, with its deeper and more favorable harbor, assumed the leadership in the industry and kept it throughout the Golden Years of whaling. She had the advantage of being a coastal seaport, making the procurement of materials, enlisting of sailors, and the loading and unloading of provisions, oil and bone, easier and faster.

As in Nantucket, the pioneers in the whaling industry and its accompanying industry, ship building, were Quakers. New Bedford citizens named Swift, Morgan, Howland, Rotch, Rodman, Gifford, Delano and Stone, were industrious and thrifty, with good business ability, and built an economy second to none.

It has been recorded that in 1857 New Bedford merchants owned 329 vessels manned by 10,000 men, with a value of over $12,000,000.00. In addition to the sailors thousands of other people were employed in supporting industries, — ship building, sail making, rope, casks, barrels, iron and candle making. One harpoon maker, James Durbee, claimed to have made and sold, between 1828 and 1868, 58,517 harpoons. There were ten other iron manufacturers in the city, each operating full time.

New Bedford lived for, and was supported by, whaling. No wonder that it has been called 'Whale City'. Its daily thoughts, conversations and activities were influenced by the whaling industry. There was a daily paper called *The Whaleman* in which was included news of the arrivals and departures of whaling vessels and whalemen; a Whaleman's Chapel in which the pulpit was built in the shape of a ship's prow and to which the minister ascended and descended by means of a rope ladder. Inns were given such names as 'The Crossed Harpoons', 'Spouter Inn', Seaman's Bethel, made famous in Melville's *Moby Dick*. There was a Mariner's Home, built in 1787 where sailors could and can, even today, get a bed, shower and breakfast, free of charge.

The Old Dartmouth Historical Society, named for the first ship launched in New Bedford, maintains the Whaling Museum on Johnny Cake Hill. Here is housed, it is said, the largest and most complete display of memorabilia and artifacts pertaining to whaling in the country.

The Whaling Museum houses a remarkable collection of scrimshaw, figureheads and sternboards, whaling implements and paraphernalia, a fully equipped whaleboat, portraits of captains and ships owners, primitive oils showing whalers in foreign ports. There is a bonus attraction of an accurate half scale model of the square-rigged whaler, *Lagoda,* which visitors may board. The original *Lagoda,* a 122 foot bark, was owned by Jonathan Bourne of New Bedford and sailed from this port for forty-eight years. Interesting, too, that it was mentioned in Richard Henry Dana's *Two Years Before the Mast.*

The Whaling Museum is open daily during July and August, Monday through Saturday 9 to 5 p.m., Sundays 1 to 5 p.m. Remainder of the year closed Mondays, Thanksgiving, Christmas, New Year's and Easter Sunday.

Salem

Situated sixteen miles northeast of Boston on Massachusetts Bay Salem is the second oldest town in Massachusetts, the first, of course, being Plymouth. It was an important commercial center for a period of over fifty years, reaching its height about the time of the War of 1812. During this time its merchants had practically a monopoly of the East India and China trade.

Yankee ships and sailors were able to win the leadership in the commerce of the world against foreign competition, particularly that of England and France, through native enterprise, brains and seamanship.

This type of man, however, evolved through two hundred years and seven generations of seafaring stock, whose knowledge and experience was gained sailing over here-to-fore uncharted expanses in search of the whale.

Whale fishery out of Salem was secondary to the import-export trade which was carried on by Salem merchants and captains, but they did maintain a respectable whaling industry and, in 1837, twelve whaleships departed from her harbor bound for the whaling grounds of South America, the Indian Ocean, the Atlantic, South Atlantic, and the Pacific.

In 1799 a group of Salem captains and supercargoes (business managers) organized "to assist the widows and children of deceased members, to collect such facts and observations as tended to the improvement and security of navigation, and to form a museum of natural and artificial curiosities, particularly such as are to be found beyond the Cape of Good Hope or Cape Horn." Qualification for membership demanded captains and supercargoes who had sailed around either or both of these Capes.

The collections accumulated slowly, being mostly parochial in character, but in 1907 the Field Museum of Chicago gave Peabody Academy the great collection of whaling material exhibited at the World's Columbean Exposition in 1893. Collected mostly in Nantucket and New Bedford, whaling materials of all types, — models, implements, scrimshaw, paintings, logs and records were arranged on the whaler *Progress,* towed to the Great Lakes and exhibited at the Exposition.

Soon after this important gift was made the name of the museum was changed to the present one, in honor of a Salem born benefactor and great philanthropist, George Peabody.

The Peabody Museum is probably the largest marine museum in the United States, if not in the world, and features the most extensive display of whaling memorabilia. It is open every day from 9 A.M.-5 P.M., on Sundays and holidays from 2-5 P.M. (closes at 4 P.M. from November 1-March 1 and all day Thanksgiving, Christmas and New Year's).

Mystic Seaport

To visit Mystic Seaport, a maritime museum on the Mystic River in Mystic, Connecticut, is to step back in time to the reality of a world in which our forebears lived and worked, a 19th century ship building community.

Many ship yards lined the banks of the Mystic River when the building of ships was at its peak, between the years 1850-1875. Mystic Seaport is located on one of these, the George Greenman and Company ship yard on Adams Point.

A description of this maritime museum in the 1972 Press Release by the Marine Historical Association, Inc. fascinates and invites the would-be marine enthusiast and scholar.

"Winding gently around the waterfront, the cobblestone and packed-earth streets are paths leading backward in time. Here are examples of homes of the period, a school, bank, chapel, general store, tavern, clock shop, apothecary and doctor's office, all needed by the people whose lives were intimately involved with the ship-building and seafaring industries."

A vibrant active museum, provision has been made for visitors to watch the artisans at work, — the weavers, sailmakers, coopers, the shipcarvers, shipsmithies and chandlers at work. There is also a gallery in the main workshop where one may observe the ship's carpenters, riggers, caulkers and painters working.

You may board the *Charles W. Morgan* (out of New Bedford), the last of the wooden whaleships which is permanently berthed here, as are several other historic vessels.

On exhibition is a unique collection of over 300 pieces of scrimshaw, ship's figureheads, rigged ship models, and oil and watercolor marine paintings.

The Museum is a non-profit educational institution and has a variety of educational programs, — mariner training, small craft building, sailing classes and hand crafts. For those students and writers doing research in the field of maritime history the G. W. Blunt White Library offers 30,000 volumes and 250,000 original manuscripts, nautical charts and ships' plans for perusal and study.

The Marine Historical Association was founded in 1929 by three Mystic area residents who wished to preserve the history of sailing ships and their accompanying industries. It has grown from one exhibit building with a small maritime collection to over forty buildings, ships and formal exhibits, and, since 1948, has been known as Mystic Seaport.

Open from April through October from 9 A.M.-5 P.M., closing one hour earlier in the winter (closed Christmas and New Year's), the Seaport admits members of the Association, children under six and members of the Armed Forces in uniform free of charge. It offers reduced rates to groups of children accompanied by adults, college students and adult groups if reservations are made in advance.

Cold Spring Harbor

The cannon on the lawn at The Whaling Museum at Cold Spring Harbor once stood on Cannon Hill on the west side of the harbor in Bungtown, (so named because the barrel factories, sail lofts, whaling company warehouses and shops were located there). It was a signal cannon and was used to announce the appearance of a Cold Spring Harbor ship as it cleared the west end of Lloyd's Neck so that the villagers could gather down at the wharf in time to greet their relatives, friends and sweethearts.

During the Golden Years of whaling Cold Spring Harbor was a thriving seaport and the Cold Spring Whaling Company sent out nine ships to every ocean in the world in search of whale oil and bone. The town was bustling with the activities connected with whaling, creating jobs and livelihood for hundreds of families.

The Whaling Museum Society, Inc. was organized in 1936 by a group of Cold Spring Harbor citizens who were interested in preserving the maritime heritage of the community.

The Whaling Museum is located on Route 25A, once Bedlam Street, so called, it is said, because of the riotous behavior of returning whalemen on their first nights back in home port after months away on whaling expeditions. Dedicated to the whaling industry the Museum houses implements used by the whaling ships' mates, carpenters, sail makers and coopers. Here is displayed a fully equipped whaleboat; a mounted lower jaw of a young sperm whale, complete with forty-two teeth.

One can also view one of the finest collections of sailors' knots that can be seen anywhere, consisting of actual examples of some 700 weaves, working splices and knots. There is a definitive collection of over 400 pieces of scrimshaw of practically every form of the whaleman's folkart. A collection of navigation instruments and a display of local documents, including whalemen's shipping papers, logs, account books, stamps and letters, give real and tangible meaning to the water colors by Comm. E. C. Tufnell R N (Ret.), of the nine Cold Spring Harbor whaleships, *Alice, Edgar, Huntsville, Monmouth, N. P. Tallmadge, Richmond, Sheffield, Splendid* and *Tuscarora*.

Open Thursdays, Fridays, Saturdays, Sundays and National Holidays from June 15-September 14 from 1-5 P.M. the Whaling Museum also welcomes groups by advance notice.

Sag Harbor

"The hollow resonance of the Cooper's hammer, the ringing clang of the Smithy's sledge, the boisterous shouts of the roustabouts and the rumbling of wagon wheels — are gone; all relegated to the same fog-shrouded past that guards the secrets of the whaleships and their now almost extinct race of valiant seamen.

The former busy home port of the early square-riggers has become a sheltered haven for the white and gilded pleasure craft of yachtsmen."

Clother Hathaway Vaughn writes thus in *The Sag Harbor Whalers.* Presently a village of about 2,600 people with several small industries and a marina which now caters to pleasure craft, Sag Harbor during the busy whaling years, was the home port of more square-rigged sailing ships sailing for foreign ports than the port of New York.

Sag Harbor on Long Island, New York, was duly constituted a port of entry and so named in the Act of Congress in 1790. Local ship builders laid the keels of most of the ships that put to sea from Sag Harbor in search of whales. The majority of their captains were townsmen or from neighboring communities; the crews were local, although they often picked up extra sailors at ports at which they called, — Fiji Islands, Kanaka, Malaya, Portugal, among others.

Over 500 whaling expeditions were completed from this Long Island port in an industry which reached its peak in 1845. Pioneered by a brig named *Lucy* which made her first voyage in 1775 and returned with 300 barrels of oil, Sag Harbor reached a maximum of sixty-three vessels in its fleet and twelve large firms in the shipping business.

Many interesting "firsts" are attributed to the Sag Harbor port. Captain Mercator Cooper sailed the whaleship *Manhattan* into the Bay of Jeddo in 1844 and was the first American to establish friendly relations with the Japanese people. In 1851 the bark *Martha II*, George S. Tooker, Captain, carried the first American Consul to Japan.

Captain Royce sailed the bark *Superior* through the Bering Strait into the Arctic in 1848, the first ship to accomplish that passage.

The whaleship *Cadmus,* owned by Mulford and Sleight of Sag Harbor, brought General Lafayette from France to this country in 1777. Another well-known name, that of James Fennimore Cooper, was connected with Sag Harbor whaling, as a "share" owner of several of their whaling ships.

Many lives and ships were lost in the pursuit of whales, and countless suffering and hardships endured. In July 1866 the ship Pacific, Smith French, Captain, was lost in the waters off Bering Island. The third mate and five sailors fought their way through the Arctic seas for two months in an open boat only to discover, upon arriving at Hakadaki, that the rest of their ship mates had been picked up by another Sag Harbor whaleship shortly after the Pacific had foundered.

Whaling artifacts and memorabilia of Sag Harbor's prosperous years are now displayed in the Suffolk County Whaling Museum. Housed in a mansion believed by many to be the most beautiful on Long Island, and built in 1845 for Benjamin Huntting, owner of many Sag Harbor whaling ships, the authentic whaling exhibits reside with and compliment the beautiful furnishings of the period.

The Museum was first opened in 1936 under the auspices of the Sag Harbor Historical Society. It was chartered by the University of the State of New York in 1942 and was given its present title, Suffolk County Whaling Museum. Open from May 15 to September 30, week days from 10-5, Sundays 2-5 P.M., the Museum welcomes visits by children, especially when accompanied by parents and teachers. School children are admitted free when accompanied by their teachers.

XIII   The Art Of Recognizing Old Scrimshaw

The bulk of scrimshaw in existence today is preserved by marine museums, hoarded by collectors, or treasured by descendants of the original artists. Formerly of interest only to marine enthusiasts, artists and historians, the art work of the Yankee scrimshander has become increasingly popular and correspondingly hard to come by.

There are several reasons for the growing interest; — its unique quality — the fact that sailors from New England and the Eastern seaboard hunted whales thousands of miles from home, and expressed their experiences and thoughts through their handiwork; their ability to etch on the surface of and to manipulate the crude materials available to them; the limited amount of scrimshaw and its corresponding increase in value.

Scrimshaw was collected and exhibited by marine museums because of its relationship to the sea and the whaling industry. About 1960 it became apparent that here was a limited product, that genuine scrimshaw was executed only during those years when the whalers were at sea, engaging in an industry that lasted for a period of roughly one hundred years. Its uniqueness, its limited supply and lack of availability makes scrimshaw a sound investment, — one which can only increase with the years.

If you are a serious and dedicated scrimshaw collector you have already established your own criteria for identifying genuine old scrimshaw. For the beginner or casually interested collector, certain signs of early techniques and age may be welcome.

The fact that a whale's tooth may be yellowed, off-white, or slightly "used" looking, does not necessarily mean that it has age and is, therefore, the product of a scrimshander at sea a hundred or more years ago. Teeth, or any ivory, yellows when exposed to the sun and weather over a period of time. A look of age may also be acquired by dipping the ivory in tea or machine oil. A yellow-ish cream color is found on nearly all genuine old pieces of scrimshaw, however.

Sperm Tooth With Patriotic Scene – creamy ivory color, irregularity of thickness and density of etching, patriotic theme, lack of artistic talent, – all are signs of age. Author's Collection.

The themes used by the whalemen were more or less standard and may be categorized briefly, patriotic, historical, marine, nostalgic. With few variations scrimshanders portrayed the flag, historical figures and occasions, views of well-known ships and coast lines, their own experiences while on whaling expeditions, and sketches of home and women-folk.

The art of the scrimshander at sea can be identified by the impression made by his tools, Working with a jack knife, sail needle or nail implements which would grow dull with use, the sailor would have to sharpen them periodically, thus varying the width and depth of the etching. These variations can be felt by the sensitive fingers of a knowledgeable collector, or determined by a jeweler's glass.

The bulk of scrimshaw executed at sea was outlined in black, — lamp black, soot from the exterior of the iron try-pots hanging over the open fire, Tar, used for caulking hull and deck seams, was handy and plentiful, — diluted until almost water-thin it was rubbed into the incisions. India ink was also used, when it could be obtained, offering faster drying and an opportunity for speedier evaluation of the appearance of the finished product.

Rubbed into the incisions in the ivory or bone, the contrast of the black on white brought into relief the highlights and shading of the art work. Sometimes tobacco juice was used and gave a mellow sepia effect.

Fids – pins used to open rope strands to splice – Courtesy Heritage Plantation of Sandwich/TFA

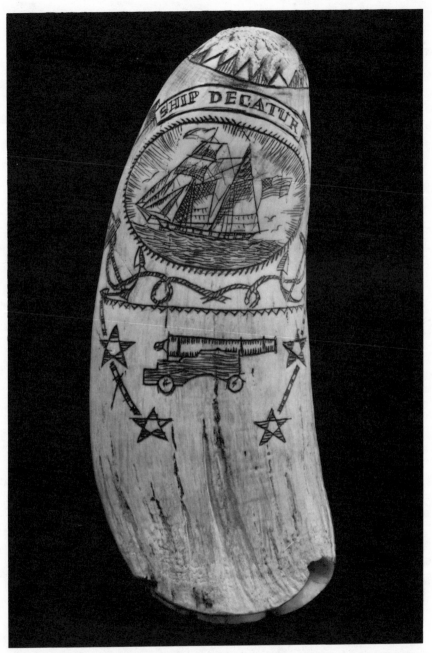

Ship Decatur – scrimshawed likeness of Ship Decatur, a privateer named in honor of Stephen Decatur, a Commodore in the U.S. Navy in the War of 1812.

The teeth done in color are few and hard to come by, generally being executed by those sailors who traveled to the South Seas area where berries, leaf and bark juices were available. At this point, however, the men who had been ship bound for so many weeks and months put their artwork aside and pursued other interests.

The real rule to follow in exploring and selecting scrimshaw of the 18th and 19th centuries is to know your antique dealer and accept his recommendations (although even antique dealers are known to have been duped). Generally, however, he has verified his material to the best of his ability, and searched its background, and offers you the benefit of his findings. He takes these necessary steps because the future of his business and his reputation in the antique field depend on his knowledge and integrity.

Lawrence E. Vienneau, Jr. at work – fineness and delicacy of lines, great amount of detail, make it necessary to use optician's glass. Courtesy Lawrence E. Vienneau, Jr.

XIV   You, Too, Can Be A Scrimshander

All kinds of American folk art are being revived, — primitive painting, painting on glass and velvet, pottery, weaving, crewel, knitting, metallurgy, scrimshaw, — art forms which our forebears performed either of necessity or for decoration.

Scrimshaw, the primitive art of the Yankee whaleman, is, in the strictest sense, etching or carving on ivory. Interest in scrimshaw is being pursued despite a growing scarcity of whales' teeth. To compensate for this lack of whale ivory, elephant and walrus tusks are now being used, also old pieces of ivory, such as piano keys, the handles of old knives and forks, old buttons, pieces of mother-of-pearl, clam shells, abalone, beef bones, lobster claws, — all are being decorated by the modern scrimshander.

The smaller articles can be fashioned and decorated into jewelry, a popular subject, which includes pins, brooches, earrings, pendants, rings, cuff links, tie clips, and key chains.

Larry Vienneau is a present day scrimshander. Hunched over a five inch whale's tooth, he will work three full days etching hundreds of tiny lines required to make a scene two inches square. His father is a dentist, but only the fact that he works on teeth does Laurence E. Vienneua, Jr. follow in his father's vocational footsteps.

Instead of a drill, the eighteen year old Duxbury (Mass.) High School senior uses a stencil blade, and the teeth he decorates are whales' teeth. His work is already recognized as museum quality by the fact that one of his decorated pieces is now owned and displayed in a museum of American art in France.

Recovering from a broken neck, incurred when diving into

a swimming pool at the Cardinal Cushing School For Exceptional Children where he was a volunteer worker in the summer of 1970, Larry looked about for something to do. He was interested in art and decided to try his hand at scrimshaw. After considerable practice he found the work fascinating and satisfying.

Much of Larry's work follows the whaleman's art and depicts whaling and marine scenes. One six inch tooth includes a highly detailed scene of a whaling ship, two whaleboats with men in position to strike a whale, and a whale, throwing off sea spray, rising out of the water.

Last summer, etching in a window in a Nantucket gift shop, this young artist earned enough money to pay his tuition and expenses at art school for the coming year. The bulk of his earnings come from etching small teeth and ivory disks to be sold as charms and jewelry. They average $7.00 to $10.00 apiece and are popular with the tourists. The whales' teeth bring about $100.00.

Larry feels that scrimshawing as a full time business could become drudgery, but as an avocation it gives him an opportunity to express his artistic talent and be remunerative besides.

You may be interested in trying your talents in this type of art work. Various steps and procedures, if followed faithfully, will give you satisfying results and a sense of accomplishment.

Present day whale ivory comes from Norway, Japan and Portugal. The Norwegian sperm and killer whale ivory, when delivered, is dirty, yellow and rough. Many hours of painstaking work go into sandpapering, smoothing and polishing these teeth to prepare the surface for etching. When you have finished this type of scrimshaw, however, you have duplicated, as nearly as possible, the article produced by the early whaleman.

To condition such a tooth, use wet or dry sandpaper #300, graduating as you work, to #600, polishing finally with fine steel wool, then emery cloth, and a final rub on your blue jeans. (The sailors used chisels, sharkskin, and the seat of their pants).

Those who do not want to go to the trouble of beginning with such raw material, and wish to get on with the design, will find the teeth imported from Japan and Portugal already smoothed and polished, and ready to decorate. If you prefer the 'aged' look, dip the ivory in warm tea for a short period of time.

Many modern scrimshaw artists work with incising tools specifically made to their design, and measurements that fit their hand. Miss Althea Macy, tenth generation descendant of Thomas Macy, one of the purchasers of Nantucket Island, is one of these. A superb creative artist in sculpture and scrimshaw, Miss Macy demands exacting tools for her craft.

According to Mr. Robert Lavery, teacher of scrimshaw in the Adult Education class on Cape Cod and in the Barnstable and Yarmouth schools, the ubiquitous jack knife is still a popular and effective tool. For the beginner scrimshander, however, he offers other suggestions, ordinary implements which may be near at hand, — old dental tools, sharpened crochet hooks, a mechanical drawing pencil with a chuck in which old victrola needles or darning needles may be inserted, a carbon or diamond-tip stylist, or an Exact-O knife, — all will serve your needs adequately, and when handled correctly, will give satisfactory results.

If you have talent and are artistically inclined, you may want to sketch or draw your own design. Take into account the shape and size of the article to be etched and choose a subject that is in keeping with the material used, both in theme and suitability. Proportion, balance and perspective are important, just as they are in any painting, drawing or etching.

The old designs and patterns used by the whalemen are still popular subjects and seem created specifically for ivory and whalebone, — sailing vessels with sails full or furled, ladies gowned in fashions copied from Godey and Leslie magazines, a whale, whaling scene, a harpooner about to strike. Patriotic themes, dear to the sailor thousands of miles from his native shores, are often used, — the flag, the eagle, shields, the figure of Liberty, political and popular personalities. All are concrete examples of a way of life during the whaling era.

When you have chosen your subject, outline the design in pencil, and, if there is a large amount of detail or overlapping lines, seal the drawing with thin shellac, or hair spray, so that it will not be blurred or erased as you work.

Grasp your incising tool firmly and work with quick light strokes; you can cut them wider or deeper later when you have determined where you want shaded, or more pronounced, sections.

When the etching is finished to your satisfaction, trace indelible India ink, non-soluble ink, or charcoal into the incisions (if charcoal is used it will be necessary to seal it). Any blurring or spill-over may be wiped off by rubbing at once with a hand-size, folded piece of brown paper bag or with quick short strokes with a damp cloth.

You do not need to be unusually artistic to be a modern scrimshander. Few whalemen were first-rate artists, yet their portrayals of life around them, no matter how crudely done, have left us with a pictorial account of the whaling industry and the times in which it flourished. When we observe their handiwork we feel their sense of accomplishment and fulfillment in expressing their thoughts through their art. You will find the same satisfaction in your art work.

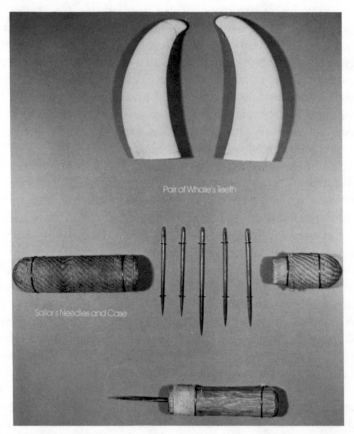

Needle Holder – whalebone holder for needles which were used not only for mending sails but often used to execute scrimshaw. Courtesy Heritage Plantation of Sandwich/TFA.

Conclusion

The causes of the decline of whale fishery were many and varied, — the destruction of so many whaling vessels, used as The Stone Fleet in blockading Charleston Harbor during the Civil War, — the Gold Rush in California in 1849 when many sailors jumped ship, — the increased cost of ships and outfitting them for longer journeys, and the uncertainty of the market when they returned, — the financial crisis in 1857, — the disasters in the Arctic in 1871, — the invention of a machine to make thin steel, — but the biggest blow of all was the discovery of oil. The opening of the first oil well in Pennsylvania in 1859 sounded the death knell of the whaling industry.

The Golden Age of Whaling, with all its excitement, romance and tragedy, has become history, as scenes viewed from afar, but the 'idle hour' work of the Yankee scrimshanders, tangible and visible evidence of their lives at sea, has become more desirable and valuable with the passing of the years.

A whale's tooth, polished and scrimshawed with a detailed whaling scene, fine and delicate as a cobweb, is as popular today as it was in the 18th and 19th centuries. Although a by-product in its day, scrimshaw, the primitive art of whalemen, bears witness to those dangerous and laborious times, and is acclaimed by artists and historians alike as true American folk art.

The End.

Cover Illustration – A dramatic moment in whale taking – portraying a boatheader, poised dangerously in prow of whaleboat, ready to plunge lance in whale's tail to sever nerve and immobilize his adversary. Author's Collection.

The Pilot House ®

Original

SCRIMSHAW KIT

© 1971 The Pilot House

There are several excellent scrimshaw kits available, all of which employ one's creative talent, and, when finished, will provide an authentic piece of scrimshaw.

One which we particularly like is singularly adapted to the beginner craftsman. It is the "Original Scrimshaw Kit", compiled by Frank Martin.

This kit is comprised of an engraving pencil, drawing ink, protractor, practice board and a genuine ivory locket with silver chain. Detailed, line by line instructions present, when finished, an engraving comparable to those inscribed by Yankee whalemen of the 18th and 19th centuries.

Less than $10.00, the "Original Scrimshaw Kit" is available at your local book or craft shop, or you may order directly from: The Pilot House, Dept. SB, Route 6 at the Narrows, Wareham, Massachusetts 02571.

992-8330

More Museums Which Have Important Whaling Artifacts and Memorabilia

1. Bath Marine Museum, Bath, Maine
2. Boothbay Regional Historical Society, Boothbay Harbor, Maine
3. Dexter Historical Society, Dexter, Maine
4. Penobscot Marine Museum, Searsport, Maine
5. Strawberry Banke, Portsmouth, New Hampshire
6. Cape Cod National Seashore, Wellfleet, Massachusetts
7. Cape Cod Pilgrim Memorial Association, Provincetown, Massachusetts
8. Cohasset Maritime Museum, Cohasset, Massachusetts
9. Heritage Plantation, Sandwich, Massachusetts
10. Kendall Whaling Museum, Sharon, Massachusetts
11. Falmouth Historical Society, Falmouth, Massachusetts
12. Marblehead Historical Society, Marblehead, Massachusetts
13. Marine Museum at Fall River, Battleship Cove, Fall River, Massachusetts
14. Mattapoisett Historical Museum and Carriage House, Mattapoisett, Massachusetts
15. Donald G. Trayser Memorial Museum, Barnstable, Massachusetts
16. Lighthouse Museum, Stonington, Connecticut
17. Milestone Village Museum, Boston Post Road, Darien, Connecticut
18. Monument House, Groton, Connecticut
19. Newport Historical Society, Newport, Rhode Island
20. Rhode Island Historical Society, Providence, Rhode Island
21. Oysterponds Historical Society, Orient, New York
22. Museum of the City of New York, 1220 Fifth Avenue, New York City
23. New York State Maritime Museum, South and Fulton Streets, New York City
24. South Street Seaport Museum, New York City
25. Johnson Whaling Collection, Princeton, New Jersey
26. Smithsonian Institution, 1000 Jefferson Drive, S.W., Washington, D.C.

Suggested Additional Reading

If, from reading *Yankee Scrimshanders,* you have become interested in the fascinating subject of whales and whalemen, and wish to pursue it further, here is a suggested list of informative and/or entertaining books which you will enjoy.

1. *Whale Ships and Whaling* : Albert Cook Church
2. *Yankees Under Sail* : Edited by Richard Heckman
3. *Moby Dick* : Herman Melville
4. *The Cruise Of The Cachalot* : Frank T. Bullen
5. *The Great Age of Sail* : Edita Lausanne
6. *History of the American Whale Fishery* : Starbuck
7. *The Long Harpoon* : Arthur Watson
8. *The Ship Ann Alexander of New Bedford* : Clement Cleveland Sawtell
9. *Scrimshaw at Mystic Seaport* : Edouard A. Stackpole
10. *Scrimshaw – Folk Art of the Whalers* : Walter K. Earle
11. *John F. Kennedy – Scrimshaw Collector* : Clare Barnes, Jr.
12. *Whale Fishery of New England* : William S. Sullwold Publishing
13. *Follow The Whale* : Ivan T. Sanderson
14. *Nantucket Odyssey* : Emil F. Cuba
15. *Nantucket* : William Oliver Stevens
16. *Nantucket Argument Settlers* : Harry B. Turner
17. *Ships and Sailors of Old Salem* : Paine
18. *Pursuing The Whale* : John A. Cook
19. *Bertha Goes Whaling* : Bertha Boyce
20. *Blue Water Men and Other Cape Codders* : Katharine Crosby
21. *Three Bricks and Three Brothers* : Will Gardner
22. *Mattapoisett and Old Rochester, Massachusetts* : Mattapoisett Town Comm.
23. *Scrimshaw and Scrimshanders* : E. Norman Flayderman
24. *The Provincetown Book* : Nancy W. Paine Smith
25. *Mark Well The Whale* : Frederick P. Schmitt
26. *Whaling Wives* : Emma Mayhew and Hough Whiting, Henry Beetle
27. *She Blows! And Sparm At That* : William John Hopkins